Period Costume for Stage & Screen

for Stage & Screen

Patterns for Women's Dress, Medieval — 1500

Period Costume

JEAN HUNNISETT

for Stage & Screen

Patterns for Women's Dress, Medieval — 1500

ILLUSTRATIONS BY KATHRYN TURNER

PLAYERS PRESS, Inc.
P. O. Box 1132
Studio City, CA 911614-0132

Period Costume for Stage and Screen: Medieval — 1500

PLAYERS PRESS, Inc.
P.O. Box 1132
Studio City, CA 91614-0132

Jacket illustration: Lady Macbeth, BBC Television, designed by John Bloomfield, 1970.

Editor: William-Alan Landes
Pattern Lay-out: Chris Cordero
Production Associate: June Heal

Library of Congress Number: 95-50302

Photo and illustration copyrights have been acknowledged throughout the text. We have tried to locate all copyright holders, but if an omission has occurred please notify the Publisher and we will try to rectify any error.

Simultaneously Published in:
Australia, Canada, U.K., U.S.A.

Printed in the U.S.A.

Hunnisett, Jean.
    Period costume for stage & screen. Patterns for women's dress, medieval - 1500 / Jean Hunnisett ; illustrations by Kathryn Turner.
        p.   cm.
    Includes bibliographical references and index.
    ISBN 0-88734-653-7 (alk. paper)
    1. Dressmaking--Patterns. 2. Actresses--Costume. 3. Costume--History--Medieval , 500-1500. I. Title.
TT520. H933 1996
646.4' 7804' 0902--dc20   95-50302
                                                                        CIP

CONTENTS

Pattern List   1

Plate List   2

Introduction   3

Part One:

TECHNIQUES OF COSTUME MAKING

1. Interpretation   7
2. Sewing Techniques   11
3. Taking Measurements   27
4. Fabrics   31
5. Draping A Toile   35
6. Making A Basic Dress   49
7. The Fitting   53

Part Two:

PATTERNS AND DETAIL

8. Middle Ages — 1400 A.D.   59
9. 1400 A.D. — 1450 A.D.   77

10. 1450 A.D. — 1500 A.D.   101
11. Surcoats and Cloaks   123
12. Italian Renaissance,
    15th Century   145

Part Three:

THEATRICAL PATTERN AND DETAIL

13. Interpretation of Costume
    Designs   173

APPENDICES:

14. Source Index   183
15. Bibliography   184
16. Index   185

Acknowledgements   187

Patterns

PAT		Page
1.	Cut Through Dress on Straight of Grain.	37
2.	Cut Through Dress on the Bias.	39
3.	Cut Through Dress, Princess Line Dress.	41
4.	Cut Through Dress with Square Gusset and Cut Through Side Panels.	43
5.	Cut Through Dress realised from the Bog Dress.	45
6.	4 Straight/Tight Sleeve	47
7.	Two Basic T-shaped Garments with Alternative Gussets.	71
8.	Three Alternative T-shapes with Dolman Gussets.	73
9.	T-shape with Separate Side Godets.	75
10.	T-shaped gown pattern realised form the Lady from the Luttrell Psalter.	76
11.	Basic 'V' Necked Houppelande.	87
12.	Pattern realised from the painting of the 'Arnolfini Marriage' by Jan van Eyck.	88
13.	Kirtle (Figures 60, 61, 62).	90
14.	Large Hanging Sleeve 'B' page 92 on Straight of Grain. Sleeve 'F' 93 using same head shape.	95
15.	Hanging Sleeve 'D' Two versions on S of G (a) in one piece (b) in two pieces. Page 93.	96
16.	Long Hanging Sleeve 'C' Cut on the Bias with (a) round end, and (b) square end. Page 92.	97
17.	Three Versions of the 'V' necked Bodice; Second half 15th Century.	112
18.	Skirt for above dress	114
19.	Two Flat Fronted Bodices and Partlet and two styles of half circle skirt.	115
20.	Bodice pattern realised from Victoria and Albert Museum 'Gothic Tapestry'.	117
21.	Chemise pattern realised from that in 'The Bladelin Alterpiece' by Rodgier van der Weyden.	122
22.	Surcoat pattern realised from Luttrell Psalter; Pieces A & B. Cyclas Pattern Piece D.	131
23.	Surcoat pattern realised from the brass of 'Lady Cobham'.	133
24.	Surcoat pattern realised from 'The Cerimonial surcoat of 'Queene Jeanne de Bourbon'.	134
25.	Surcoat pattern realised from the painting of Salome from van der Weyden's "The Beheading of John the Baptist'.	136
26.	Surcoat pattern realised from 'The Master of the Joseph Sequence'.	137
27.	Half-circle Cloak with (A) No neck shape, (B) With neck shaping gathered or pleated across the shoulder.	143
28.	The Surcoat and Bodice pattern realised from; 'A & B' 'The Birth of Venus' by Fra Carnevale. 'C' Bodice from 'Jason and Medea'.	157
29.	The Tabard pattern realised from 'The Visitation' by Ghirandaio.	159
30.	Chemise pattern realised from that of 'Venus' in 'Mars and Venus' by Botticelli.	160
31.	Man's sleeve pattern realised from 'The Adoration of the Magi' by Veneziano.	163
32.	Man's sleeve pattern realised from a painting of a fashionable young man by Domenico de Bartolo.	165
33.	3 Sleeves realised from frescos or paintings of women depicted in Renaissance Art.	167
34.	Pattern used for the ladies corps de ballet 'Romeo and Julliet' N.Y. City Ballet designed by Nicholas Georgiadis; realised by Carol Hersee.	179

Plates

Plate		Page
1/2	La Clemenza di Tito by Mozart, showing a raked stage.	9
3/4	Fastenings/Machine Feet	10
5	Printed Velvet	26
6	Jersey moulded over a stand.	30
7/8	Woven fabric draped on half size stand.	35
9/10	Toile: Cut on straight of grain draped on stand.	38
11	Toile: Finished front and back toiles, both bias and straight on the same stand.	38
12/13	Toile: Cut on bias draped on a stand.	40
14	Toile: Finished front and back toiles, both bias and straight on the same stand.	40
15	Dress design for 'The Magic Flute' for Pamina.	40
16	On a stand in the workroom the Pamina dress.	42
17/18	Toile: Cut through dress with square underarm gusset.	42
19	Pattern from Norse Settlement Herjolfsnes, Greenland, of a Woman's dress. (After P. Norland.)	44
20	Toile: Greenland Grave dress.	44
21	Adjusting a neckline in the Glyndebourne workshop.	48
22	Annette Crosby dressed as Queen Victoria, demonstrating a piped hem.	52
23	Fitting: Jean Hunnisett with soprano Felicity Lott and wardrobe manager Tony Ledell.	55
24	Jean and Tony in Jean's cutting room.	55
25	Cuff, first half of the 13th Century.	67

Plate		Page
26/27	Toile: Dolman sleeved T-shape; Pattern 8.	72
28	Toile: Pattern 9; Lady from the Luttrell Psalter	74
29	'The Arnolfini Marriage' by Jan van Eyck.	80
30	Sample of decoration for Arnolfini dress.	80
31/32	Toile: Out and Inside of van der Weyden's 'Young Woman'.	83
33	Pattern 10. Houppeland toile.	86
34/35	Patterns 11 and 12. Arnolfini toiles.	86
36/37	Pattern 13. Kirtle toiles.	89
38	Pattern 15. Toiles: Hanging sleeve on straight of grain.	91
39	Pattern 16. Toile: Hanging sleeve on Bias.	94
40	Designs for Pelleas et Melisande.	98
41	The Donne Triptych by Hans Memlinc.	105
42	Toiles: Three variations on the 'V' necked bodice. Pattern 17.	111
43	Boned Stomacher used to cut flat front bodices over.	113
44-6	Toiles: Bodices on Pattern 19.	113
47/48	Toile: Gothic Tapestry bodice. Pattern 20.	116
49	Toile: Lady Luttrell surcoat. Pattern 22.	130
50	Toile: Lady Cobham surcoat. Pattern 23.	132
51/52	Toile: Pinned and finished toile for Joseph Sequence surcoat. Pattern 26.	135
53-5	Toile: Half circle cloak on half sized stand.	139

Plate		Page
56-9	Toiles: Bodices on Pattern 28.	156
60	Toile: 'The Visitation' on Pattern 29.	158
61	Toile: 'Venus" chemise, on Pattern 30.	158
62	Samples of template and sleeve dagging.	161
63	Unfinished dresses for the ballet 'Romeo and Juliet'.	172
64	Design for Banquet costume (see 65).	173
65	Janet Suzman in costume designed for banquet in Shakespeare's 'Macbeth'.	173
66	Design for Sleepwalking costume (see 67).	174
67	Janet Suzman in sleepwalking scene for Shakespeare's ' Macbeth'.	174
68	Design for sleepwalking costume (see 69).	175
69	Grace Bunbry in sleepwalking costume for the opera 'Macbeth'.	175
70/71	The mother Gabriel Lloyd in 'Churchill's People'; 'The Peasants Revolt'.	176
72	Margaret Paston Gemma Jones for 'Churchill's People';'A Wilderness of Roses.'	177
73	Design for the corps de ballet for 'Romeo and Juliet'. Pattern 34.	177
74	Unfinished dresses for the ballet 'Romeo and Juliet'. (See Plate 63.)	178
75	Front and back view of the dress for 'Marie' for 'Simon Boccanegra' by Verdi.	181

Figures (See Source Index page 181.)

INTRODUCTION

The development of style throughout the period covered by this book is an extremely slow affair when compared with the twentieth century. Existing costumes and textiles are rarely seen by the general public and the pictorial references are not as easily interpreted as that of the sixteenth century. But the more familiar this period becomes the easier it is to understand.

I hope, from a theatrical point of view, to stimulate those working in costume interpretation to a better understanding of a period which is so distant, as well as so different from our own. There are many ways to approach both the look and cut of costume, my aim is to help those involved in the production of clothes, to 'read' and translate the source material or costume design, into a three dimensional garment.

The illustrations have been chosen using as reference, paintings, monumental brasses, sculptures and drawings many of which are easily available in current publications. Some show the theatricality of a fashion, and some the progression of shape and style. They have been dated by cross checking the most reliable sources available. However, I am not a dress historian and those working on re-creations should go back to the originals in churches, libraries, art galleries and museum textile departments for a first hand look.

For the patterns, I have interpreted both specific examples, from source material, and the development of various styles of a particular fashion. I have done this in my own way as if interpreting designs for a play, but at the same time trying to keep the feeling of the period. For instance, for the fitted kirtle I have given a variety of ideas, some based in fact and others which are created to fill the gaps in the factual information.

I also discuss the interpretaion of costume designs for television by John Bloomfield, and for ballet and opera, in the theatre, by Nicholas Georgiadis, and John Gunter. Costumes for performance must be made so that they are comfortable to wear and easy to maintain. The making of costumes of this period can be achieved mainly by modern dressmaking techniques, as there is very little of the boning used in more structured periods.

When using my method of draping a toile to make a pattern, as opposed to making a pattern draft— it is the actual measurements of the artist, the design and the width, type and quality of the fabric that will determine the details. Unless it is crucial that the measurement should be exact, most measurements in this book are approximate.

Another dilemma in this type of book, is how accurate the conversion of the measurements from metric to imperial should be, so unless otherwise stated the conversions of the measurements are approximate. On the whole with this period, where fabric is not fitted tightly to the body, errors of up to a half centimetre can easily be tolerated.

Over the last 40 years I have cut and made costumes for a multitude of period dramas and operas for television and film, as well as for ballets, operas and straight plays for the theatre. I also indulged in a side line of clothes for strangely shaped static models for wax work exhibitions. I have cut costume for periods ranging from Greek tragedy to Elizabethan drama and eighteenth century romps, to adaptations of staid Victorian and

Edwardian novels and exhibitions. I also ventured into futuristic costume for a Sci-fi television series. After being a freelance costumier for most of my working life, I retired in 1992 after seven years cutting costumes of many periods and styles at Glyndebourne Opera in East Sussex.

It has been my privilege to have dressed many great actresses, dancers and singers, in the designs of many talented designers.

PART ONE:

Techniques of Pattern Making

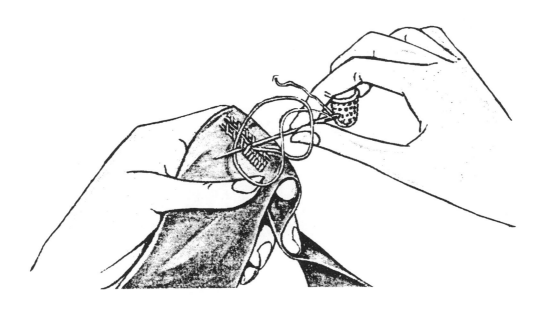

1. INTERPRETATION

The interpretation of costume from any source is a difficult concept to explain. It is not just copying from the design, but for example, with strict period clothes, getting the fabric of a skirt distributed round the waist so that the fullness falls in such a way, as to get both the right shape, as well as making the garment easy to move in. During the 1970's and 80's many directors and designers in the theatre set period productions in symbolic or modern sets and costumes instead of those for which they were written. But in the 1990's the pendulum seems to be swinging back, and designers are again looking for good period shapes.

Period Costumes for television and film are apt to be more conventional than those for the theatre. They fall into two main categories. Firstly, the silhouette must be good enough for the period to be recognised when the costume is seen in long shot. Secondly, for close-up shots, the detail round the head and arms is critical. If possible, no visible machine stitching or zips, etc., should be seen in periods when they have not yet been invented, as such details look out of place and are magnified many times on a big screen.

In the theatre fine details are not quite as important, except in very small theatres where the audience is very close to the stage. Decoration must be bold enough to be seen from the front, but must not get out of proportion with the garment. Level hem lines are essential, although very difficult when the performers are working on a raked stage. If there is any aspect of a design that is a problem, it should be discussed with the designer at toile stage, to see how it can be solved within the confines of the design, before putting scissors into the cloth.

Clothes of this period consist of different lay-ers. The chemise, which could have been more easily washed or cleaned, is worn under the kirtle. The sideless surcoat is worn over the kirtle. Unless the top fabric is textured or a brocade the audience sees only large areas of plain cloth, which can appear uninteresting. When choosing fabrics try to find different textures as well as colours for the various garments and their linings to make the costume look more interesting. A good example is the painting by Rogier van der Weyden, 'The Magdalan Reading' in the National Gallery, London (Figure 57) which show three different textures in the skirt area. The houppelande is made of green cloth, bordered with fur and turned back over the knees, showing that it is also lined with fur. The kirtle worn under it, is made in a rich gold brocade.

When dressing any character try to keep these various layers separate, even if parts of the under garments are hidden from view. This will make the end product more realistic. If there are puffs around the armhole and down the sleeve as in many Italian Renaissance paintings, do not skimp by putting false chemise sleeves and necks on the under bodice or catching them into the garment itself. Make a separate chemise, but when dressing, the costume will need to be put on more carefully, so that the puffs can be arranged to look good each time. Most artistes will take the trouble to dress properly if asked. The separate chemise can then be washed more frequently, which keeps the linen looking fresh and the costume off the body. The inside of the costume will also stay cleaner during a long run, than when each puff is stitched in as a separate item.

When making costumes for this period, especially those for a ballet such as "Romeo And Juliet", specifically the ball, the costumes must be functional as well as the correct shape for the period used by the designer. The fullness round the waist of the long skirts — as those in the Italian Renaissance chapter or as the design by Nicholas Georgeardis in the last chapter of this book — must be placed so that the skirt is relatively easy to pick up to allow freedom of movement. Too much fine or slippery fabric bunched across the centre front will create a problem for the dancer.

For easy research try to build a collection of postcards - most art galleries and museums now sell a wide range of postcards based on their collections. The student looking for visual help, and lacking the finance to buy Museum catalogues or books containing good reproductions, will find buying postcards is a more economical way of acquiring visual information. Arrange them in chronological order, so that the development of the various styles of costume can be seen. Collect different paintings of the same date, by both the same and other painters and look at the variations in the details of sleeves or necklines (Figure 1.) Also compare the difference in styles between the colder northern countries of England and Flanders and the warmer republics of Florence and Venice in the south. Make sure that the artist is using the style of dress of his own period, and not going back in time, as in some of the paintings by Mantegna for example.

Study the paintings of artists who are helpful to the costume maker - a good example is Rogier van der Weyden 1399-1464 who gives a clear account of the Nederlandish dress of his day, enabling the keen observer to work out the cut. In this way you will soon learn to 'read' the paintings, which in turn will help you to 'read' a design.

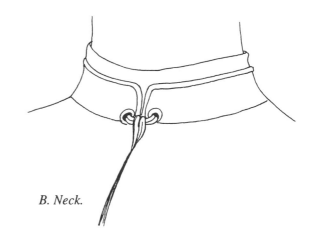

B. Neck.

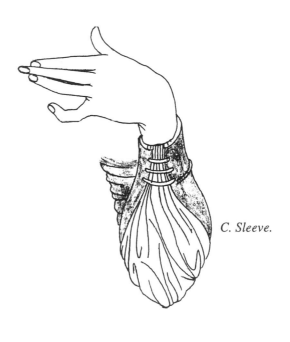

C. Sleeve.

A. Neck.

Figure 1. Examples of sleeve (C) and neck (A and B) details from paintings of the Italian Renaissance.

Plate 1. (Above.)   Photo © Guy Gravett

Plate 2.   (Below.)   Photo © Guy Gravett

Plates 1 and 2. These photographs from the 1991 Glyndebourne Opera Production of 'La Clemenzo di Tito', directed by Nicholas Hytner and designed by David Fielding, show a steeply 'raked' stage. All the artist went barefoot to assure a good grip when moving up to down the stage. The robes worn in this last scene were made in grey slub silk. After cutting, they were hung to allow the fabric to drop, after which they were levelled in such a way as to appear neither too long nor too short on either the up or downward slope of the rake. The (Top) photograph shows, centre of the picture, the main characters Ashley Putnam as Vitellia and Philip Langridge as Tito, Diana Montague, to the far right, as Sesto with the Glyndebourne Opera Chorus. The (Bottom) photograph shows Philip Langridge as Tito and the Glyndebourne Opera Chorus.

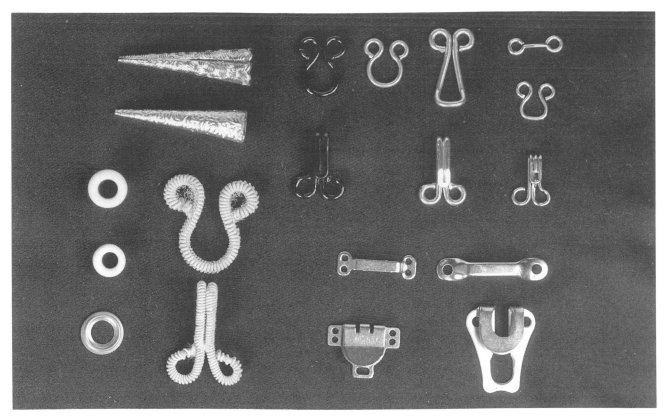

Plate 3. Eyelets, Aiglets, Fur Hooks, Mantle Hooks and Loops, Skirt Hooks,
Trouser Hook and Bar, No. 3 Hook & Bar, Loop.

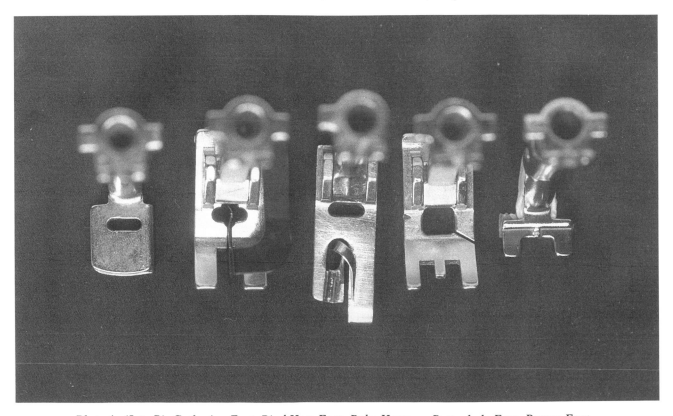

Plate 4. (L to R) Gathering Foot, Bind Hem Foot, Baby Hemmer, Buttonhole Foot, Button Foot.

2. SEWING TECHNIQUES

Aiglet. The metal tag on the end of a lace. These can be bought in specialist shops. They take the form of a small metal cone, usually patterned, and can be stitched onto the end of a lace; alternatively dip the end of the lace or fabric rouleau into Evostick, push it into the aiglet and hammer it flat. (Figure 2.)

two pieces of fabric together right sides facing — machine together round the outer edge leaving a gap on one side — trim **the allowance** to 6 mm (^{1}/4 in) clip off the corners — and turn through to the right side and press. (Figure 3.)

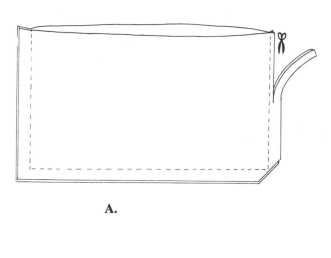

A.

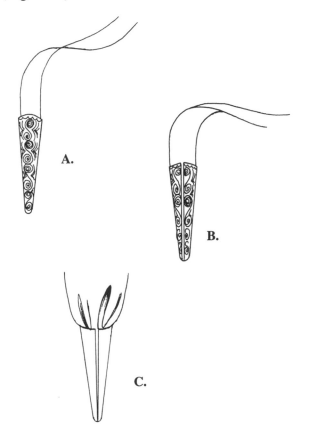

Figure 2. Aiglets. A. Front. B. Back. C. With Rouleax.

Baby Hemmer. This attachment is available for most makes of sewing machine. It will turn a 3 mm (^{1}/8 in) hem on most thicknesses of fabric from organza to calico. (See Plate 4, third from left.)

Bag out or Turn out. A method of lining or facing a collar or the front edge of a cloak. Put the

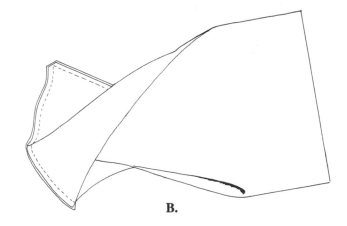

Figure 3. Bag out. A. Inside out. B. Turning.

Balance Mark. A mark, such as a notch on a commercial pattern, to assist in putting the pattern together accurately. Place marks at several points along the length of the seam, varying the number of marks on different seams. e.g. 3 centre back, 1 side seam, 2 side back seam etc. (Figure 4.)

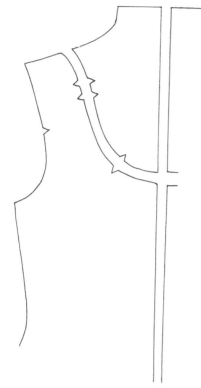

Figure 4. Balance Marks; 3 on the yoke, 1 on the armhole.

Bias. Fabric cut on the cross or the bias. To find the true cross, fold the selvedge *(the warp)*, across the width *(the weft)* of the fabric. The resulting fold of the fabric should be the true cross.

Bias binding. Used for binding edges usually about 12mm ($^1/2$ in) wide and made from cotton. Three qualities are available: (1) soft in feel but closely woven, (2) stiffer but coarser, (3) a very firm bias used for binding corsets available from corset sundries suppliers. Also a gadget is available in the shops which will make bias binding from a strip of any suitable bias fabric.

Binding In. To finish the edge with a bias binding, with no binding showing on the right sides. (Figure 5 a/b.)

1. With right sides facing, machine the binding along the fold onto the seamline of the garment and trim off any surplus allowance.

2. Press the binding to the inside of the garment. Clip the allowance and ease or stretch the bias when binding a curve.

3. Fell the binding on to the inside of the garment, without letting the stitches show on the face.

Binding Over. To finish an edge with a matching or contrasting fabric, either for decoration or a flat finish. (Figure 6 a/b.)

1. Machine on the finished line e.g. neck etc. and trim close to this line.

2. With the right side of the garment facing,

Machine Line

A.

Figure 5. Binding In. A. Machine line. B. Fell the binding down.

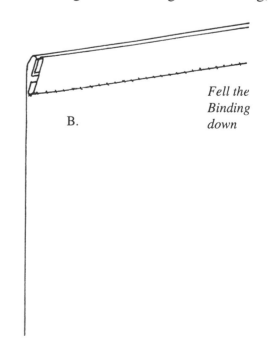

Fell the Binding down

B.

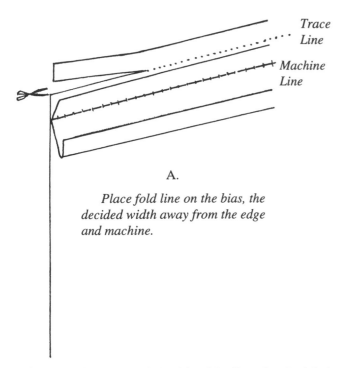

A.

Place fold line on the bias, the decided width away from the edge and machine.

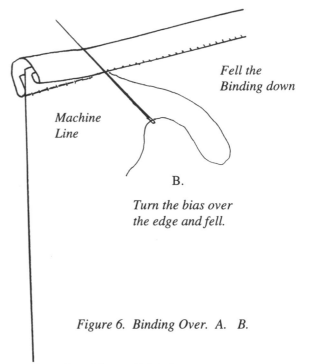

B.

Turn the bias over the edge and fell.

Figure 6. Binding Over. A. B.

place the fold line of the bias binding the decided width away and machine on along the fold, easing or stretching it round the curves.

3. Turn the bias over the edge of the fabric and press. Fell it on to the wrong side just above the stitch line.

Bodkin. A blunt needle with a large eye used for threading ribbon or elastic.

Bones. see 'Rigilene'.™

Button Foot. Made for attaching buttons on a zig-zag machine. Very useful for stitching on hooks and bars, etc. It is usually necessary to drop the feed on the machine.

Buttonhole. This is an operation which is usually incorporated into the sewing machine. Buttonholes can also be done by hand.

Cartridge Pleating. A method of fitting a large amount of fabric into a small space. It can be used for purposes such as yokes, sleeves and skirts. If you are inexperienced you will need to do a small sample to find out how deep the pleats need to be, for example:

If a skirt is 3.65 m (4 yds) wide divide it

into 8 = 45 cm (18 in).

If a waistband is 71 cm (28 in) divide by 8 = 9 cm (3 1/2 in).

This means that a medium wool fabric would need 18 x 1.2 cm (1/2 in) deep pleats into every 9 cm (3 1/2 in), each pleat taking 2.5 cm (1 in) of fabric. If the fabric is fine silk you may need 36 x 6 mm (1/4 in) deep pleats each taking 1.2 cm (1/2 in) of fabric. The period, the design or the type of fabric will determine the amount of fabric in the pleating and therefore the size of the pleats. When pleating a skirt, if the pleats are more than 6 mm (1/4 in) deep they will need grading down in size at either side of the centre front, which as a rule is left flat or eased across. Depending on the waist measurement, the flat across the front can be from 6.3 cm (2 1/2 in) to 10.16 cm (4 in).

The method for Cartridge Pleating:

1. When cutting a length of fabric for pleating as well as allowing extra length for a hem, it is usual to leave 2.5 cm (1 in) to 5 cm (2 in) at the top to turn in. However if the pleating needs extra support — for example at the top of a skirt or sleeve or to thicken up pleats made in fine fabric — enough length must be added at the top to allow for a deeper fold.

2. After the seams have been joined and the

shape of the top of the work has been established, draw a line and machine along it. Leave on the required amount above this line, and neaten the edge. When the top of the pleating is shaped, as the centre front waist of a skirt, the fold over at the centre front, will cause resistance. To release this, clip with the scissors, the fold over, as far as the machine line.

3. Turn in and press and then edge stitch along the folded edge. This will strengthen the edge and act as an anchor when stitching the pleating on to a band or yoke.

4. Finish the edges of the placket opening by binding or turning them in. (see Plackets).

5. With the right side of the work facing put press fasteners on to both sides of the opening on the right side of the fabric. This will make the opening look like an inward facing pleat, which will hopefully be invisible, without it being bulky.

6. Using a very strong thread, which needs to be as long as the finished pleating, plus 30.6 cm (12 in), put a substantial knot on the end of the cotton. If the pleating is used for a skirt, and the join must look like a pleat, the knot at the end of the cotton must be on the *outside* of the fabric, but if the pleating is starting from a flat portion of a skirt, yoke or sleeve, the knot will be on the *inside* of the work. (Figure 7 A.)

7. Starting with the knot on the correct side for the work in hand, and 6 mm (1/4 in) from the top — for 1.2 cm (1/2 in) pleats — take even

stitches 2.5 cm (1 in) long, along the length of the fabric.

8. Put in a second row of thread no more than 1.2 cm (1/2 in) below the first. The distance between the rows of thread depends on the depth of the pleats, e.g. as a general rule half inch pleats, will be half an inch below, quarter inch pleats will be a quarter of an inch below.

If you are pleating a long length of fabric, work the two needles together, using the first needle for 45 cm (18 in) and then the second needle, and so on to the end.

9. Pull up the threads from *both* ends to the required length.

When finished the pleats at the waist should butt up to each other very closely, if not the pleats are too deep and need to be done again. A tape or band is needed to mount the pleats on to, what ever the purpose you are using the pleating for.

10. Cut the band the finished length of the pleating plus any extra needed for turnings, and divide the band and the pleating into equal segments, (see Quartering a Skirt) so that the pleating will fit evenly along the band when finished.

With the wrong side of the work facing you.

11. Pin the pleats evenly along the band.

12. Stitch about three times into every pleat going through the edge stitching of the pleats and the waistband. (Figure 7 B.)

If the pleating is being used for a skirt, tie the

A.

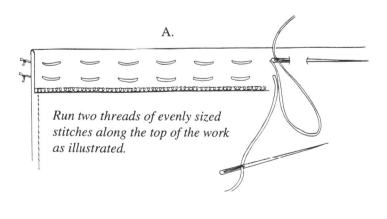

Run two threads of evenly sized stitches along the top of the work as illustrated.

B.

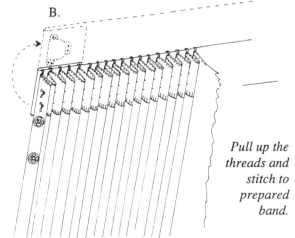

Pull up the threads and stitch to prepared band.

Figure 7. Cartridge Pleating. A. Run two threads of evenly sized stitches along the top of the work, as illustrated. B. Pull up the threads and stitch to prepared band.

threads off with a temporary slip knot so that they can be altered, and put a temporary fastening on to the waistband for fitting. If you are sure that it will fit, put the skirt on to a stand and ease out the pleating along the threads, particularly the second row, otherwise it will restrict the pleating and cause a gap at the fastening. Pass the threads through to the inside and tie them off permanently and finish the waistband.

To finish the waistband.

13. With the right side of the work facing you. Turn back the righthand side of the waistband and whip round the edges and then buttonhole on a trouser hook.

14. Turn back the lefthand side, leaving about 3.8cm (1 1/2 in) protruding, to create an inlay, whip round this and buttonhole on a trouser bar. When the skirt is fastened the pleats should be so close that the join disappears.

Diagonal Basting. Temporary slanting stitches used to hold the lining and top fabric together when mounting, especially when dealing with large pattern pieces. (Figure 8.)

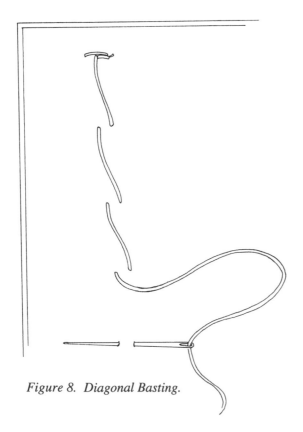

Figure 8. Diagonal Basting.

Domette. Used for interlining, quilting etc. There are two types, flat and fluffy. The latter is used for quilting.

Drill. A twill weave cotton, used for mounting a bodice.

Edge Stitch. Used on the edge of a neck or armhole etc., or in the preparation for cartridge pleating and centre back lacing. Stitch on the very edge of the seam or fold of fabric. (Figure 9.)

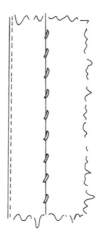

Figure 9. Edge Stitching.

Eyelets. Metal eyelets with washers are the quickest way to eyelet a costume for lacing. When buying eyelets in bulk, buy all white and either dye or paint them to match the colour of the bodice. Today many sewing machines with the appropriate gadget will embroider eyelets.

The neatest eyelets are those done by hand. (Figure 10.)

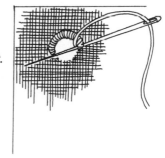

Figure 10 Handmade Eyelet.

If the fabric is coarse, iron a piece of fusible

fabric behind the hole. By placing a small wire ring or washer on the back before stitching, it will help to make the eyelet more hard-wearing. Do not use buttonhole stitch over the washer, as the bead of the stitch wears, leaving a raggy hole.

1. Pierce a hole with a stiletto, through the layers to be eyeletted. Working from the right side, overcast round the hole. Push the stiletto through the hole to open it up.

2. Take the needle to the wrong side, and now carefully overcast round the hole again, push the stiletto through to open it up again and the stitches will practically disappear. Finish off well.

To protect eyelets from wear — starting at the top; lace a ribbon or corset lace down to the bottom and then back to the top and stitch the ends firmly to keep the lace from unravelling. Do each side of the opening separately. This will take the strain of constant wear. (Figure 11.)

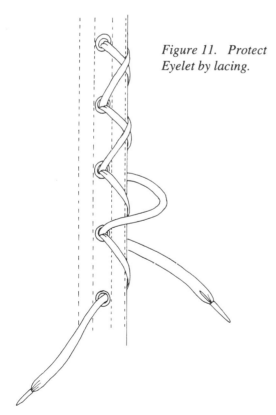

Figure 11. Protect Eyelet by lacing.

Facings. To face a neck, an armhole or hem. Cut the facing if possible on the same grain as the area being faced. Stitch it either on the right side to face in, or the wrong side to come on to the surface to make a decoration.

Fastenings. A bad fastening can mar a good costume. It is as important to get a good closure as it is to do elaborate decoration. Zips are unreliable and make very clumsy fastenings unless they are put in beautifully by hand. Invisible zips are useful in this period as they appear as a seam when put in with care, but all zips deteriorate if cleaned frequently.

'Velcro' ™, is not suitable to close a tightly fastening dress and it is difficult to get the edges to meet evenly every time.

Hooks and Eyes and Loops come in sizes from O to 3's. Size three's are used for most types of fastenings.

Mantle or military hooks and loops are useful where a strong fastening is required. They are made of stronger wire and are larger than those above.

Trouser hooks and bars; the 12 mm (^{1}/2 in) size are useful for skirt fastenings.

Fur hooks and loops are useful for fastening bulky fabrics such as fur or thick wools, which do not take any strain. They can also be used as decorative attachments through which to thread thick lacing.

There are 5 different ways to close a garment, (A) hooks and loops, (B) hooks and bars (C) hooks and holes, (D) buttons and holes, and (E) lacing, for which the opening can be prepared three different ways. On most garments whatever type of closure you are using the fasteners are best placed 3 cm (1 ^{1}/4 in) apart.

When looking at a bodice from the outside, whatever variety of a hook fastening is being used, the hooks should always go onto the righthand side, which means that for a righthanded person the hooks should be in the right hand for ease of fastening.

A. Hooks and loops make a flat edge -to-edge fastening. (Figure 12.)

1. Turn in both sides of the bodice on the line, and edge stitch. The hooks must be set so that the head of the hook is just back from the edge stitch line, catching in the bodice mounting, but not the bodice. The hooks can be oversewn round the

ends, but a professional maker usually uses a buttonhole stitch.

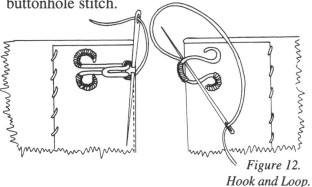

Figure 12.
Hook and Loop.

2.   Stitch on the back loops of the hooks.

3.   Catch the hook end, taking small stitches at the head of the hook pulling tightly, and finish off by stitching over these stitches. This should stop the head of the hook from sliding forward.

4.   Fell back the allowance firmly on to the bodice lining.

Put the loops so that only the tips can be seen from the outside.

5.   Stitch on the back end and catch the loop end on both sides to the edge of the bodice. The part of the loop that protrudes can be covered with buttonhole stitch in a cotton which matches the fabric. (This not only looks good, but stops the hook from sliding out of the loop.)

6.   Make and put in the inlay. (see Inlay.)

B. Hooks and bars. (Figure 13.)

1.   Put the hooks on as for A.

2.   Face back the bar side to create an inlay, or when cutting the bodice etc. cut an extra 3 cm (1$^{1}/_{4}$ in) on to the left side which can then be turned back and machined on to the centre line.

3.   Buttonhole stitch the bars along the inlay side of the stitch line.

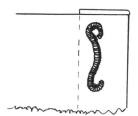

Figure 13. Hook and Bar.

C. Hooks and holes are good for a very flat closure. Make the holes first so that you can judge where to set the hooks. The holes must be placed to the allowance side of the centre line, and the hooks need to be set well back. (Figure 14.)

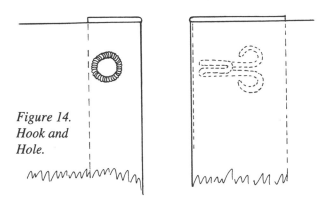

Figure 14.
Hook and
Hole.

1.   Turn in the lefthand side as for the bars and make eyelet holes by hand or machine. (see Eyelets).

2.   Put on the hooks as for A, making sure they cover the holes.

D. Buttons and Holes. To make a bodice or tunic look as if it meets edge to edge, set the buttons just onto the inlay side of the centre line. Make a shank when putting on the buttons or use a button with a built in shank. Place the button holes as near to the centre front edge as possible. They can be made either by hand or by machine.

E. Lacing. All lacing needs some type of stiffened edge if the finished fastening is going to be smooth and neat. There are three ways to prepare the edges. The first two methods are good for medieval dress, especially if the dress has a front fastening. Method (a) makes a very firm edge, with no visible means of support, Method (b) makes a finer finish, if the edge stiffening is pricked in by hand, or it can be made into a decorative feature. Method (c) is the usual way to lace the back of bodice or dress, which needs a good firm fastening that can take the strain required.

Method (a).

1.   Machine down the line of the edge that is

to be fastened. This acts as a stay stitch and is important especially if the line is shaped or off the straight of the grain.

2. Put a rigilene bone (see rigilene) on to the allowance side of the line and machine down both edges. Then turn in and press.

3. Now put in the metal eyelets *through* the bone and bodice together.

Method (b).

1. Prepare the edge as for method (a). Prick a fine cord into the folded edge. If the lacing edge does not lie flat, pull up the cord and finish the ends firmly.

2. Make hand or machine made eyelets just behind the cord.

Method(c).

For the back of a bodice, only one bone on each side is necessary, but two are needed for a corset.

1. Machine down the line. Press the allowance in, and edge stitch. Both sides of the fastening are treated in the same way.

2. Machine a second row making a channel which will hold a steel bone tightly — or if the fastening needs to curve in at the waist use a spiral bone.

For a corset, continue as follows.

3. Machine a third row, leaving a gap wide enough to take the eyelet .

4. Machine a fourth row to take a second bone.

5. Put in the eyelets either between or immediately behind the first bone, using small metal eyelets with a washer on the back.

Corset lacing can be bought in various lengths or on a large roll of approximately 200 metres or yards. Lacing can be dyed to match the colour of the fabric.

Felling or Hemming. Used where a facing is to be stitched on to the body of the garment or for felling in linings or hems.

A hem needs to be about 5 cm (2 in) deep.

1. With the wrong side facing, and starting on a seam if possible. Peel back the top of the hem with the thumb and 'fasten on' the thread on the inside.

2. Staying on the seamline catch to the inside of the garment.

3. Insert the needle through the peeled back hem again, about 0.5 cm ($^1/4$ in) below the edge, and between 12-20 mm ($^1/2$ - $^3/4$ in) along the hem and pull through.

4. Immediately above, take one thread of the garment only. At this stage if the hem is vulnerable to snagging on the ground etc., before tightening the stitch, pass the needle through the loop of thread.

Continue to end. Do not pull the thread too tight as this will pull the threads of the body of the garment and the hem will show. In these days of machined hems, not enough care is taken to stitch neat hems, especially for the stage.

Finish or Finishing. Meaning to finish the edge of a seam or hem, etc. with an overlocked, zig-zagged or overcast edge. In the tailoring trade a 'finisher' is a person who puts in the linings and puts on buttons, etc.

Flat Tacking, or Basting. Used to hold the layers of fabric together. (Figure 15.) Put a knot on the end of a single thread, take evenly spaced 1 cm ($^1/2$ in) stitches slightly to the allowance side of the trace line, cut the thread at each corner and start again on the next length. This will allow the tacks on any length to be removed, leaving all the others

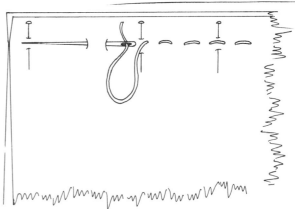

Figure 15. Flat tacking or Basting.

18

intact. Some sewing machines do a tack stitch — one stitch in two or three — which works well and saves time. Fabrics such as cotton and wool are easier to deal with than some silks and velvet. With experience, bodices can be made up just by pin tacking, which is much quicker.

Foot's width away. To machine a row of machine stitching, half the machine foot's width away, with the right hand side of the foot on the edge of the garment, or against the last row of stitching. (Figure 16.)

Gathering. Can be achieved in four ways:

1. On the machine from the right side of the fabric. Use a long stitch keeping an easy tension on the top cotton, but it must not be a loop. Put a stronger thread on the bobbin of the machine. Always put in two rows a machine foot's width apart, and gather by pulling up the strong thread.

2. Zig-zag over a piping or fine blind cord, and pull up the thread. This is a good way to pull up thick fabrics. (Figure 17.)

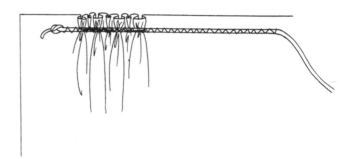

Figure 17. Gathering over a piping cord.

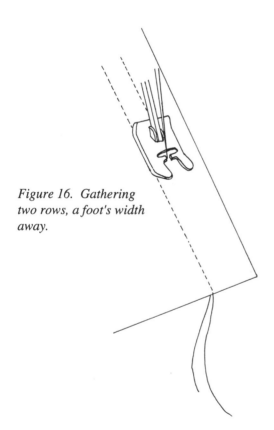

Figure 16. Gathering two rows, a foot's width away.

3. Pushing the fabric with a pin or scissor point, under the foot of the machine as you sew - good and quick for net, but needs practice.

4. On the machine using a gathering foot. This is a small square machine foot with a hole in the centre, and can be used for gathering trimmings or frills, the larger the stitch and the tighter the tension the greater the gather. Follow the instructions in the manual of the machine. If you sort out the work before you start and can keep the machine running at a steady speed, the frill will be more even than if you have to stop and start frequently. (See Plate 2. Foot 1.)

Fusible Fabrics. Fusible's can be used for stiffening all weights of fabric, as well as helping to control those which are loosely woven. Fusible canvases for tailoring are also available. Fusible fabrics such as 'Staflex' ™or 'Vilene' ™ are ironed on, usually using a steam iron or damp cloth to make them stick. To hold a difficult fabric while machining; a narrow strip can be ironed on lightly, which with handling will drop away when no longer needed.

Godet. A three cornered piece of fabric, which is let into the outer edge of a bodice or a skirt. It works as a dart in a bodice or a flare on a skirt, but with a dart or a flare the fabric is taken out to shape the garment, whereas a godet is let into a split therefore spreading or opening up the fabric. (Figure 18.)

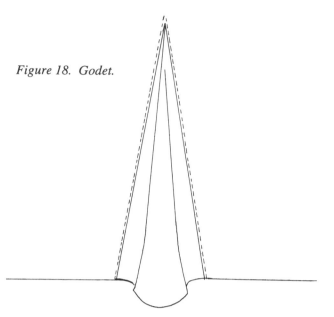

Figure 18. Godet.

Inlays. The backing down an opening and can either be cut on, as for hooks and bars, or as below a separate strip of fabric laid behind as for lacing or hooks and loops.

1. Cut a strip of fabric about 10 cm (4 in) wide *plus twice the seam allowance of the fastening,* and the length of the opening again plus seam allowances.

2. Fold in half and machine across the top and bottom.

3. Turn, press and neaten the raw edges together.

4. ***Behind Lacing or Loops:***

a. *Lacing.* Backstitch the inlay on to the allowance just behind the eyelets. Finish the edges, then herringbone it down to the mounting of the bodice.

b. *Loops.* After putting on the loops, pin the inlay to the seam allowance and finish all the edges together. Fell down this edge to the mounting of the bodice with a firm close stitch. Catch the bodice edge between the loops to the inlay. (Figure 21.)

Gusset. Usually square or diamond shaped and lets fabric and shape into a garment, usually at the underarm or the crotch. (Figure 19.)

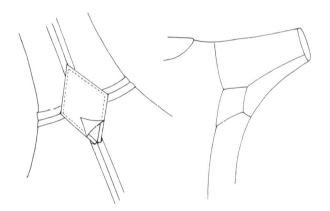

Figure 18. Gusset.

Herringbone. A progressive cross-stitch which is worked from left to right. Used for putting in neck frills, fill-ins or cuffs, etc. (Figure 20.)

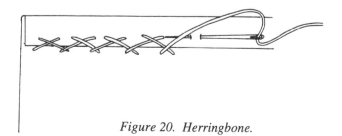

Figure 20. Herringbone.

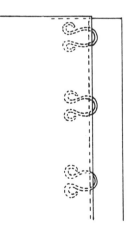

Figure 21. Inlay.

An inlay for hooks and bars can be cut on to an opening by cutting the left side 3 cm (1 $^{1}/_{4}$ in) wider than the right, or it can be faced back.

Interlining. (see Mounting)

Lacing. (see Fastenings).

Lining. Usually a lightweight slippery fabric which is felled into a garment.

Mounting. The process of putting two or more layers of fabric together to be treated as one - in order to support the fabric when making a bodice - a fine fabric which needs more body - and putting three layers of fabric together for quilting, e.g. top fabric, wadding and lining. This must be done very carefully and all the layers must be pressed flat with no creases. All pattern pieces of a garment should be treated in the same way. (See Making A Basic Dress, page 50.)

Nick or Ditch Stitching. Used when two pieces of a costume e.g. the bodice on to the skirt, or, the sleeves into the bodice, are put together by back stitching in the nick or ditch created by piping the edge.

For attaching a bodice to a skirt.

1. Lay the nick/ditch of the piping along the join line and pin.

2. With a strong double thread, back stitch in the nick or ditch between the piping and the bodice, taking the needle through to the back of the waistband each time, and fasten off well.

Petersham. Used for waistbands and is woven in a ribbed weave.

Pins. For general use 30 mm (1 ^{3}/16 in) are a good length for costume making.

Piping cord. Used for piping necks, etc. or for gathering by zig-zagging over it. Piping cord comes in sizes 00/1/2 fine, 3/4/5 medium and 6 thick.

Piping. Used a lot in theatrical dress making, and is the usual way to finish the bottom of a bodice, or an open neckline. The bodice is usually piped with its own fabric, but a contrast can be used. It must be cut on the bias and care must be taken to get the width exactly right. One layer of fabric is usually enough, but if it is fine use it double, folding it in half along its length and using the folded edge to stitch down on to the bodice. (Figure 22. A—C.)

To pipe round the bottom or neckline of a bodice.

1. Measure off the piping cord allowing an extra 2.5 cm (1 in) at either end.

2. Cut a strip of the fabric to be used for the piping, on the bias.

3a. If the fabric is to be used single, fold it along its length off centre one third, two thirds.

3b. If the fabric is to be used double, press it in half along its length and then, as above, fold it off centre, one third/two thirds, the two thirds being no more than 1 cm (^{1}/2 in) wide.

To make the two ends of the piping easier to finish:

4. Square off the end of the bias and turn in between ^{1}/2-1 cm (^{1}/4 -^{1}/2 in) depending on thickness of fabric. Place the cord in the lengthwise fold, leaving 2.5 cm (1 in) of cord sticking out. Machine along to within 2.5 cm (1 in) of the end using a zip or piping foot on the machine. The next stage is easier if you have machined a line round the bottom of the bodice or neckline and have trimmed away any surplus bulk created by the seams, *except the side seams which must be left intact to allow for any alteration that may be needed at a later date.*

5. Put the stitch line of the piping on to the stitch line of the bodice, and machine together stopping 2.5 cm (1 in) from the end. Trim the surplus fabric to fit and fold in as at the beginning and continue on to end, leaving the cord sticking out. I find all piping easier to do without either pinning or tacking.

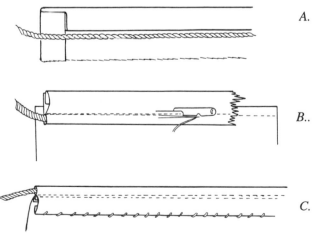

Figure 22. A. Laying the cording into the fold. B. Machine on to garment. C. Finished wrong side or inside.

21

6. Trim away any surplus fabric, turn in the edge and fell to the bodice.

7. Pull up the slack in the cord. At the second fitting if the neck is still slightly loose, pull up the cord again to make it grip the neck edge.

8. Stitch down the ends of the cord.

Placket. A fastening in a seam or split for the closure of a skirt or loose fitting dress. There are three ways to prepare a placket: (A) a placket in a cartridge pleated skirt; (B) a continuous placket; (C) a flat closure using an inlay.

Method (a)

It is not necessary to put a placket into a cartridge pleated skirt, (see Cartridge Pleating) the edges can just be overlocked or zig-zagged and then turned in 5 mm (^{1}/4 in) and machine, alternatively both edges of the opening sides can be bound over with a 5 mm (^{1}/4 in) binding. Care must be taken to finish the bottom of the opening very strongly, this can be done by stitching backwards and forwards at right-angles to the seam.

Method (b) (Figure 23.)

A running placket can be used for a petticoat, full skirt, or loose fitting dress particularly when the skirt opening is subject to rough handling, as neither the placket nor the skirt will tear down when it is caught by a foot in a quick change. The length of the opening can be decided on at the fitting. The width of the placket and size of the allowance will vary with the type of garment, and the thickness of the fabric. But it never needs to be more than 3 cm (1 ^{1}/4 in) wide.

1. Cut a stripe of fabric twice the length of the opening, and double the width of the finished placket, plus the allowances.

2. Press it in half length-ways. If the fabric is thick try to use a selvedge for the inner edge and press accordingly.

3. If the placket is in a seam, clip the seam allowance at the bottom of the opening. If it is made in a split, make a small dart at the end

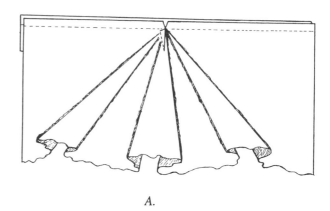

A.

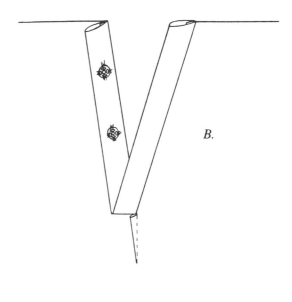

B.

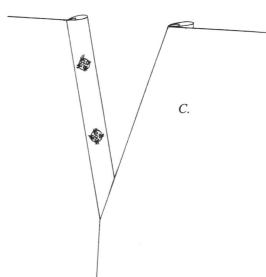

C.

Figure 23. Continuous Placket. A. Lay the strip and the skirt right sides together. B. Inside. C. Outside.

of the split, and clip the fabric at the top of the dart.

4. With the placket strip underneath, lay the strip and the skirt right sides together. *Using the width of the skirt allowance or the width of the dart as a guide.*

From the inside of the garment, machine from the top to the bottom machining backwards and forwards across the seam at the bottom to strengthen it, then continue up to the top of the second side. (Figure 23 A, Opposite.)

5. Trim and press the allowance flat towards the placket strip. Adjusting the width of the placket and turning in the allowance to meet the machine line, re-press the outer fold. Machine or fell down the inner edge by hand.

6. Press the finished placket, folding back the right-hand side, leaving the left-hand side flat, then put on the poppers. Two are usually sufficient, the first about 5 cm (2 in) from the waist and the second half way between this and the bottom of the placket. If the waist fastening has been put on properly, and the bottom of the placket clipped and pressed well, to take out any kinks during the making, this is a very satisfactory method of closure.

Method (c) (Figure 24.)

A skirt placket which needs to look like a continuation of a seam, often on the side front. Most successful when used for fine wools or linen. All corners and turnings of the placket must be clipped or cut back to keep it as thin as possible.

1. Machine a stay stitch along the seam allowance lines on both sides.

2. Press the seam open.

3. Prick an edge stitch down the hook side and then treat the hook side as for Hooks and Eyes (see Fastenings). Remember to set back the hooks to get a good closure.

4. The bar side of the opening — For the inlay cut a strip of fabric as long as the opening, and twice the finished width, plus the allowances all round it.

5. Fold the inlay in half length ways, and overlock, zig-zag or bag out one end, keeping it as flat as possible. Turn and press.

6. Place the inlay in position down the seam allowance line on the bar side of the opening, with all the raw edges together, and machine.

7. Press all the allowances towards the garment and neaten them together, catching the bottom of the inlay across the seam allowance.

8. Stitch the bars about 3 cm (1 1/4 in) apart, as close to the seam as possible, or do hand made bars by buttonholing round three or four strands of cotton. When this closure is finished it should be very flat and look like the continuation of the seam.

Pressing. When pressing try not to get the imprint of the allowance on the right side. When dealing with any fabric which is prone to this, slip a piece of card under the allowance before touching it with the iron. With fine or plain fabrics it is best to use the toe of the iron, placing the

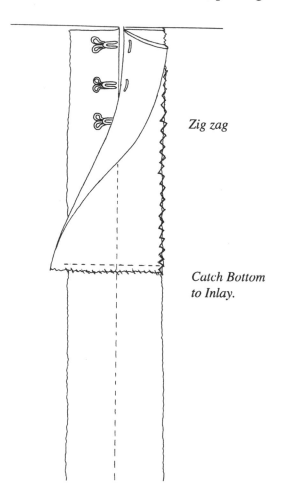

Zig zag

Catch Bottom to Inlay.

Figure 24. Placket to look like a seam.

seam along the edge of a sleeve or skirt board.

1. Press flat — press all seam allowances one way.

2. Press open — open the seam allowance and press.

Quarter the skirt. A method of distributing the fabric evenly round a waist band, whether the fabric is pleated, cartridge pleated or gathered.

1. Mark the waistband at each quarter.

2. Mark the quarters on the skirt fabric, by first marking the centres front and back. To get the balance of fullness between the front and back, find the half way point and move it 15 cm (6 in) forward, thus making the back at least 30 cm (12 in) longer on each side than the front.

3. When gathered match the quarters of the skirt to those marked on the waistband.

The same method of distributing large amounts of gathered or pleated fabric can also be used to put a frill round the bottom of a skirt or decoration round the edge of any garment. Divide both pieces of the work into even segments, sort out the fullness in each segment of the gather or frill, pin it on to the garment and machine or hand stitch them together.

Reinforcing a corner. Stops fray when clipping into a corner, e.g. when putting a gusset into a piece of fabric not using a seam. (Figure 25.)

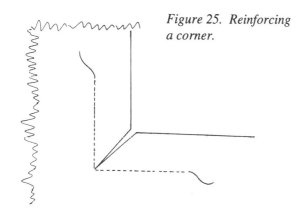

Figure 25. Reinforcing a corner.

1. Machine 1 cm (¹/2 in) along the seam line to the corner, lift the foot and realign the machine.

Repeat on the second angle of the corner.

2. Clip into the corner, with sharp scissors, close to the machine line.

Rigilene. The trade name for a continuous nylon boning, composed of five or six nylon filaments. It is used by straight stitching on each side of the bone, directly onto the mounting fabric of a bodice, or into the placket. (see Fastenings — E. Lacings). Use by cutting the boning to the correct length, passing the end through a candle flame, which will melt the filaments together, thus stopping them from fraying. Caps to put over the ends are now available in shops, but this is not as flat as candling the ends.

Scissors. Three pairs of scissors are ideal: a small pair for snipping and unpicking; a pair of cutting out scissors or shears and a pair of paper scissors.

Stay tape. 6 mm (¹/4 in) wide made in linen, can be used for example to hold a V-neckline which is not cut on the straight of grain. 6 mm (¹/4 in) India tape can also be used.

Stiletto. A small sharp pointed tool with a round shaft, used for piercing holes when hand making eyelets.

Tailor's Chalk. Used for marking fabric. Comes in white, black, yellow, blue and red.

Tape. India tape. For general use, e.g. hanging loops, covering waistbands, etc. A woven tape from 6mm-2.5 cm (¹/4-1 in) wide. Buying in 25 m (25 yd) rolls is more cost effective than small amounts.

All tapes come in black and white.

Tracing paper. Comes in packets usually containing 3 colours and is used to trace or mark pattern pieces with a tracing wheel.

It can be used in two ways:

For tracing on to one pattern piece only, glue the paper on to a piece of cardboard.

When used for tracing two facing pieces of the fabric, fold or use two sheets glued together, and sliding between the two layers or fabric, tracing both left and right sides at the same time.

Tracing wheel. Used for tracing a dotted line when using tracing paper. The more expensive metal spiked wheels work the best and are a good investment.

Tucking foot. Used when tucking fine fabrics, using a twin needle on the sewing machine. It has grooves on the under side which hold the fine pin tucks in place whilst stitching.

Twill tape. Used for corsets, or when a stronger tape is required. It is woven with a herringbone twill weave.

Waistband. (see Petersham or Webbing)

Wax (bees). Used for waxing cotton. This deters the cotton from knotting and breaking.

Webbing. Used for making harnesses to hold in place draped garments or waistbands as an alternative to petersham which is usually woven from a man made fibre, whereas webbing is usually cotton and more pleasant to wear.

Wheel Piece. A triangular shaped piece of fabric that is added at the selvedge edge to extend a large piece of skirt or cloak pattern. In the period we are dealing with most pattern pieces are large, and will usually need a wheel piece to get the width at the widest part. (Figure 26.)

Yard sticks and Squares. Yard, or metre stick, and 50 cm or 18 inch ruler are extremely useful, also a plastic or metal square. Morplan in Great Titchfield Street, London produces a very useful plastic square called a 'Pattern Master' designed by Martin Shoben. It is produced in both imperial and metric and incorporates a curved edge and french curve. The Imperial Square is marked from centre outwards, on its straight edge, in inches and eighths, and inwards at quarter inch intervals for two and a half inches as well as for one inch round its curved side. The Metric Square is marked in the same way with metric equivalents. It also has pivot holes for grading and sizing a curve.

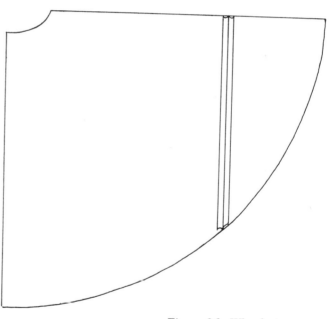

Figure 26. Wheel piece.

Plate 5.   Velvet printed with a metalic bronze. A Renaissance design.

3. TAKING MEASUREMENTS

Measuring the person for whom you are about to make a costume is the first, and one of the most important, jobs whatever the period or design.

Whether you work in metric or imperial is immaterial, above all you must be accurate. Always take the measurements yourself, over bra and pants, with your actress wearing no shoes. Do not use an old worn tape as they are apt to stretch.

When you take measurements, you are looking at two things: (a) the structure and (b) the shape of the body.

The most foolproof method is to use certain bones in the skeleton as guide points. As you work through the list, look for problems such as protruding shoulder blades; round, dropped or uneven shoulders; or the way the neck sits on the shoulders. If the muscle from neck to the shoulder is prominent creating a sloping neck, you will have problems fitting a high collar.

Look out for the long body and short legs, or the short body and long legs on a tall person. Take note of these problems during the measurement stage so that when you come to use them you will have confidence that the shape you are creating on your stand is the correct one.

I have used the following measurements successfully for many years, but with experience you will add to them or formulate your own system.

BUST. Take this over the fullest part of the bust, keeping the tape well up at the back. Make a mental note if the back muscles are well developed — this is quite common now that weight training has become so popular.

UNDER BUST. This should be taken over the diaphragm or, if the garment is to be high-waisted, wherever the design or period of costume dictates the waist should be. For dancers and singers you must also take a second measurement with the chest expanded.

WAIST. Make sure this is right, ask the actress if the tightness of the tape measure feels right — some people like a tight waist, others loose.

HIPS. Take this over the widest part of the hip and tummy, keeping two fingers inside the tape measure for ease. Note how far down from the waist you take the measurement.

I find length measurements taken from the nape of the neck more reliable than those taken from the shoulder. When taken from the shoulder, depending on the system used, they can be taken at the side of the neck or the centre, or even the edge of the shoulder if taken by someone with little experience.

NAPE TO WAIST BACK (N-W-B). From the bone at the back of the neck to the waist. If you have difficulty in finding the waist, put a tape round the waist and measure to that.

NAPE TO WAIST FRONT. Over bust point. (N-BP-W-F). The first part of the measurement is taken from the bone at the back of the neck, round the side of the neck, down to the bust point, then to under-bust, and down to the waist. Alternatively straight down from bust point to waist. This measurement will give you the bulk shape of the breast and the nape to bust point will tell you if a person is high or low slung.

NAPE TO SHOULDER TO ELBOW TO WRIST. (N-Sh-E-Wrt). This is taken with the arm bent and raised to just below shoulder level. Start at the bone at the nape of the neck, measure to the nob of bone on top of the shoulder, then to the elbow bone and finally to the wrist bone. At this point, if possible, establish the length of the sleeve.

WAIST TO GROUND. (W-G) Taken at the side front from waist to ground with no shoes. If you have difficulty finding the waist use the tape trick again, also try to establish the length of the skirt. This may change but it is at least a starting point. Larger ladies often have a dropped waistline at the front and are high at the back. When faced with this problem, take front, back and side measurements.

NAPE TO GROUND. (N-G). Using the same bone at the back of the neck, measure to the ground — the end of the tape should just brush the floor.

Compare the N-G with the N-W-B added to the W-G to make sure there is not too much discrepancy — 2.5 cm (1 in) either way is alright. If the nape to ground measures more you are dealing with round shoulders, or if less, a hollow back, or you have made a mistake.

NECK. Measure round the base of the neck. If your design has a high collar take a second measurement where you expect the top of the collar to be.

ROUND THE ARM

UPPER ARM. Measure round the fullest part of the arm.

FOREARM. As above. For very tight sleeves a measurement round the elbow may also prove helpful.

WRIST. Measure just below the wrist bone and also to wherever the sleeve is to end.

These measurements and chart are suitable when making a pattern by means of a toile, and are quite sufficient for most periods of costume. The skeletal measurements will give you the structure of the body, and the round measurements the shape. With experience you will be able to visualize the shape and size of a person from a set of measurements. If you draft dressmaking or tailoring blocks you will need a different system which will not be covered in this book. (See Bibliography.)

The countries of Europe use Metric measurement. In the U.S.A. the Imperial system is still predominant. In the U.K. metric is taught in school, but I find that the units of measurement in Imperial — inches, feet, etc.— and their multiples are easier to visualize.

Measurements come in from all over the world, so I like to keep Metric and Imperial measurements side by side in the chart.

A TYPICAL MEASUREMENTS CHART
(Figure 27.)

Name:_____

Production:_____

Date: _____ Height._____

		cm	in
A	Bust	_____	_____
B	Under bust	_____	_____
C	Waist	_____	_____
D	Hip	_____	_____
F-C	Nape to Waist-back	_____	_____
F-A	Nape to bust point	_____	_____
A-B	” to Under bust	_____	_____
B-C	” to waist	_____	_____
F-J	” to shoulder	_____	_____
J-K	” to elbow	_____	_____
K-L	” to wrist	_____	_____
C-M	Waist to Ground	_____	_____
F-M	Nape to Ground	_____	_____
0	Upper Arm	_____	_____
P	Forearm	_____	_____
L	Wrist	_____	_____
N	Neck	_____	_____

Figure 27.

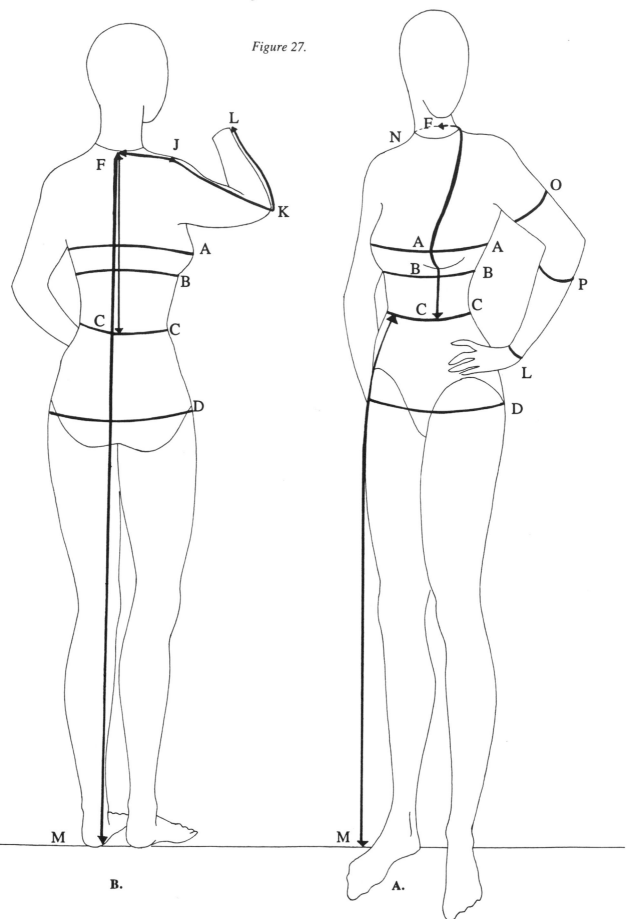

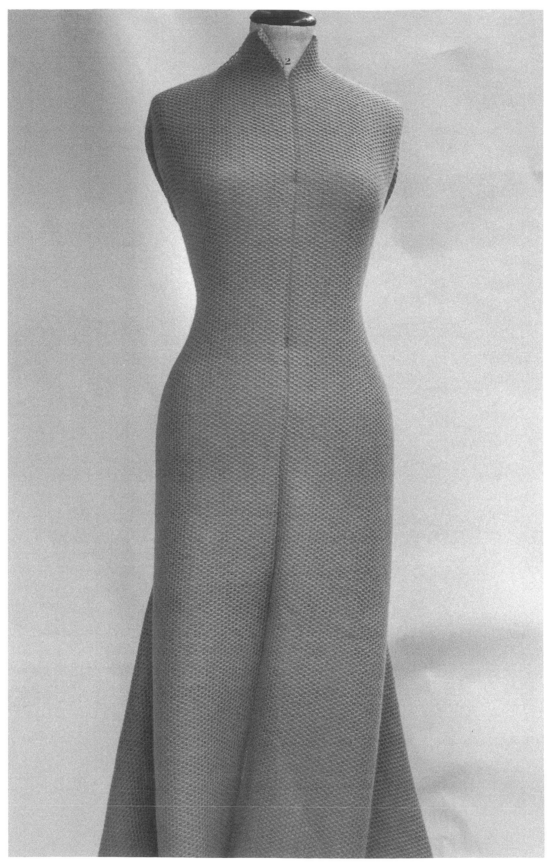

Plate 6. Textured Jersey moulded on the stand.

4. FABRICS

The choice of fabric for this period of costume is very important, owing to the size of the pattern pieces and the sparseness of the decoration. Most of the ladies' outer garments are longer than ground length, and must be lifted to enable the wearer to walk. They must therefore drape and hang well, but must not be too bulky when a top and lining fabric are made up together. They need to be varied in texture and colour — the medieval period was very colourful, with strong reds, blues and greens and more subtle shades of pinks and russets, as well as sumptuous cloth of gold and spectacular brocades.

Costumes made in natural fibres are more durable than man-mades, they clean and wash better.

Most of the costumes of this period use a lot of fabric, work out your meterage/yardage carefully.

1. Taffeta and brocades — can be used for grand costumes or the stiffer styles of Renaissance Italy.

2. Light Wool -– such as crepes or wool taffetas and those having good draping and moulding quality for the lighter medieval garments.

3. Heavy Wool — such as those made from thicker yarns, light velours or twill weaves, for cloaks and heavier outer gaments.

4. Cotton — of various weights, voile, batiste, lawn, or cambric, etc., for chemises and general under pinnings. Calicos and sheetings, of all weights, can be dyed and used for rough garments.

Fine cottons, voiles or soft silk lend themselves to soft drapery as opposed to a bouncy fabric which will balloon out. If the fabric is antique pleated it adds texture to the finished garment. Pleaters who still do this type of pleating are difficult to find, but if you have the courage you can do it yourself. For example small amounts are used for sleeves seen in Italian paintings.

WATCH POINTS

a. Wet the material and pleat the lengths by stroking rough pleats in to it with your fingers.

b. Twist the fabric squeezing the water out and wrap it with strips of fabric or tie it round at intervals. If it is a long skirt length it should twist up like a hank of knitting wool.

c. It can be dried naturally which may take days, or better still bake it in a drying oven used for drying dyed fabric or wigs. But — A SAFETY WARNING — do not leave it overnight in a domestic oven on a low gas, as a student of mine did, or you may cause a fire.

I suggest that before you try to pleat a long length, that you experiment on samples of a variety of fabrics, and avoid a disaster. A FINAL WARNING — pleating done in this way is not permanent.

5. Jersey and knitted fabrics — can be used for slinky theatrical styles. It is easy to mould these more stretchy fabric to the figure, although they are apt to drop. (Plate 6.)

6. Velvet or velveteen — in glowing colours, gives a sumptuous look to any period. According to the Oxford English Dictionary it was first recorded in England in the Wardrobe Accounts of Edward II in 1320. Velvet should always be pressed on a velvet board, but most velveteens can be pressed on an ordinary ironing table.

Always try a sample before embarking on pressing long seams in any fabric.

7. Panné velvet — is much thinner than velvet, with a longer smoother pile that does not need a velvet board when being pressed. A good quality panné can look like satin or when dyed has a crushed appearance. It works very well when used as a fitted dress or when it is allowed to fall into graceful folds. It looks even better when printed with a suitable design. If it has a strong colour it looks very rich when it is printed with either a dark or metallic print that allows the lustre of the panné to shine through. (Plate 5.)

8. Linen — in various weights for underwear, shifts and aprons. Pure linen has the drawback that it creases easily.

9. Silk — The term silk covers a multitude of weaves and weights of cloth, such as Noiles - Organza - Chiffons - Habutai - Japs - Taffetas - Foulards - Slubs and Satins, to name a few. The lighter weight silks are suitable for underwear, whereas taffetas and some satins will make grander garments.

10. Raw silk Noiles — which were used during the war to pack explosives because they did not burn — come in many weights and surface textures but whatever weight they always drape well. Thin rough textured noiles make good peasant shirts and coarse shifts, the heavier weights, smooth or rough in texture, are particularly good for heavier garments such as cloaks.

11. Organza — is quite stiff and is useful for headdress veils. When used for a dress it can be moulded on the bias over a stand and steamed into shape.

12. Chiffon — can also be used for headdresses, but its main use in the context of this book is for romantic shifts and dresses for characters in a ballet such as Juliet in Romeo and Juliet.

13. Many furnishing brocades or ecclesiastical fabrics have the right type of pattern for this period, but the design of the cloth needs to be chosen carefully. They are very effective when made into the stylish, courtly gowns of the fourteenth and fifteenth centuries.

14. Raw slub silk — comes in a large range of colours including shots — meaning that the fabric is woven with the weft and the warp in different colours, creating a more lively appearance — but it does not hang well unless it is weighted round the hem.

15. There is a wide range of satins which come in all sorts of fibres. Pure silks are very expensive but have a lustre and depth of colour rarely found in cotton or man mades. Some are made in mixtures such as silk and wool or silk plus man made fibres. The weaves vary also — such as crepe backed satin which drapes, duchess which is stiff, or lingerie which is smooth and soft. It can also be woven with a double weave — which is thick, very sumptuous and very expensive. Satin comes in all widths from narrow 45 cm (18 in) for millinery or lapel facings for men's tuxedos to 1.50 m (60 in) cotton furnishing satin. Cotton satin has a good smooth finish, it is a fabric that presses well and although quite solid, it will also stretch and mould.

16. FUR— in this period was used as a lining for garments to keep the wearer warm. In many illuminated manuscripts and paintings, all that can be seen are a fluffy edge to skirts, necklines and sleeves. But the opulent as well as the practical use of fur can be seen when skirts are turned back to show a fur lining, which on the right side of the skirt, neck edge and cuffs shows as a narrow band as in the 'Magdalen Reading' and the 'Arnolfi Marriage' as illustrated in Section 9 of this book.

When using fur in the theatre, fake fur is the easiest type to use. Manufacturing methods have now made fake fur a very good imitation of the real thing, although the cheaper types can look thick

Fabrics

and woolly. New real fur or an old coat can be used, but the choice between real and fake fur will depend on the policy about its use adopted by the company for which you work.

I am not a furrier but I have had a great deal of experience with the problem of applying fur to garments. The same method of cutting out and making up applies regardless of whether the fur you are using is real or fake.

WATCH POINTS

When using any type of fur, small pieces can be patched together to make larger pieces, but with real fur make sure the pile is running the same way and look out for thin and worn patches.

Always cut from the skin side of the fur, taking care to get the pile running in the direction you need. The pile in fake furs will usually brush any way you wish.

Never just cut into the fur with a pair of scissors, as this will club cut the pile. Use a fur knife, or with scissors, slide the lower blade along the skin between the pile of the fur, cutting only the skin or backing and not the hair itself.

Join all the edges with either an over stitch or on a zig-zag machine. This will whip just the edges together.

When a seam has been sewn, from the right side, run a pin, stiletto or the blunt point of a scissor blade along the seam, lifting the hairs out of the stitching.

TO CUT THE FUR
First make a very precise pattern for the fur.

Cut the fur with **no** turning on the joins or any shaping, such as darts, add 1.25 cm (^{1}/2 in.) round the outside edges.

TO MAKE UP FUR
To get the nice rounded appearance on both real and thin fake furs, mount it onto a layer of cotton or terylene wadding which must be cut to lie within the 1.25 cm (^{1}/2 in.) turning cut onto the fur.

Diagonal baste the wadding and the fur pieces together with stitches of about 5 to 7.5 cm (2 to 3 in.) long, the larger the pieces the longer you can afford to make your stitches.

Zig-zag a 1.25 cm (^{1}/2 in.) tape round the outside edge of the fur, on the skin side, mitring all the corners.

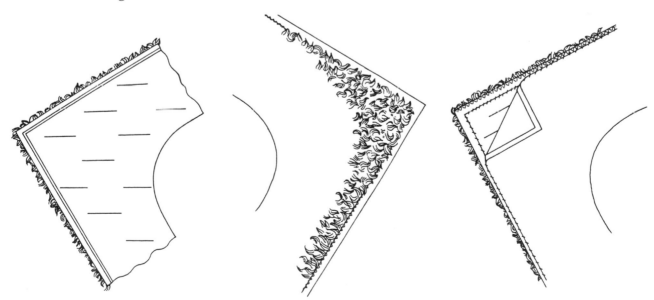

Figure 28. Diagonal Basteing. Tape turned in.

Figure 29. Zig-Zag tape onto edge of fur.

Figure 30. Lining felled onto fur.

Turn in the outer edge to fit the garment, and glue it down to the skin or backing of the fur or herringbone it onto the wadding. Make sure that the folded edge of the garment meets the zig-zag stitching on the tape.

If the fur is for items such as collars or cuffs, cut and make-up a lining and fell the folded edge onto the stitch line of the tape. If it is itself a lining for a sleeve or skirt then lay the fabric onto the fur and, after basting and fitting them together carefully, fell as above onto the stitch line of the fur.

Using this method of making up the fur means that at no time are you hand sewing into the pile of the fur which, with a long piled fur, can be very tiresome as the hair will knot itself into the cotton.

It is a good idea to wax the thread when hand sewing fur.

Fabric of the medieval period was woven in both wide and narrow widths. The narrow widths dictated the cut of some garments. For example, the width of the fabric used for the Golden Gown of Queen Margareta in Uppsala Cathedral is 60 cm (23 5/8 in) wide. The dating for this dress in the revised 1994 publication is between 1403 and 1439 and researched by Agnes Geijer, Anne Marie Franën and Margareta Nockert (see Bibliography.) In London, silk and woollen fabrics have been excavated mainly from refuse pits and river side sites, where it is thought they were thrown as rubbish. Researchers Elizabeth Crowfoot, Frances Pritchard and Kay Staniland write about the surprising variety and complication of the weaves of woollen cloth including woven stripes and checks in *Textiles and Clothing — Medieval Finds From Excavations in London No4*. Also described is the method of fulling, raising and shearing the woven cloth, perhaps many times to get a close, soft and supple velvety finish, such as the cloth seen in the woman's dress in Jan Van Eyck's 'The Arnolfini Marriage'. Fine gauzes and patterned silks from Italy and the Orient have also been found, but not linen as this does not survive in the same conditions.

There are many fabrics that can be used for the periods in this book but, as always, there is no substitute for going into a shop and feeling the weight, hang and moulding qualities of a fabric.

5. Draping a toile

As is to be expected, there are very few examples of costumes of this date in existence. Those that remain are fragile, and spread across Europe from Scandinavia to Spain. Recent conservation and research of some of these very old clothes has brought fresh thinking on the cut and detail of the construction, as with the Golden Gown of Queen Margareta and the more recent archaeological finds in England.

When cutting most periods, I do not work from a flat pattern block. I drape a toile on the stand. I like to use a Siegel and Stockman stand model 50406, as the proportions are good and the bust is not too prominent. They are made with a papier maché base which allows the pins to go into the body of the stand, unlike the fibreglass based stand on which the pins slide.

Although adjustable stands seem a good idea, they do not allow the pins to go into the stand where you need to pin, at the centres front and back. It is usually at these important points that the stand splits to enable it to be adjusted to size. When I worked, free-lance, for the straight theatre and television, I used three bust sizes of stand — 81.25 cm (32 in) — 89 cm (35 in) — 96.5 cm (38 in), but as cutter in the Glyndebourne Opera workshops I had access to stands up to size 112 cm (44 in). Anything larger than this and I borrowed a man's stand from our tailors' work shop of the right waist size, and padded up the bust and hips.

The periods covered by this book are ideal for this mode of working, but they do use a large quantity of fabric. If possible use a half size dressmaker's stand, to work out the shape of the garment. This will **not** give you an accurate

pattern that you can double in size, but it will enable you to play about with ideas, and hopefully end up with a good shape from which a pattern can be developed for a full sized dress.

Plate 7. Fabric draped on small stand.

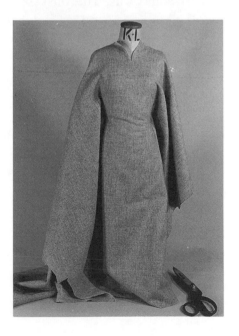

Plate 8. Fabric pinned round on small stand.

35

To make the toile the right size, repeat the shape on a full-sized stand taking it down to hip level only.

Make the toile into a pattern by drawing a pencil line along the pinned seam lines at the sides and shoulder, etc. and harden up any outer edge lines. Do not forget to put in the balance marks, these are placed at intervals along the length of the seams and above and below places where one fabric is eased onto another. I cut off all the seam allowances of the toile, so that no mistakes can occur.

Extend the skirt from the hip or waist adjusting the width of the hem at the same time. This can be done when you are making the toile into a paper pattern, or if you are confident, straight onto the fabric itself.

Before starting to cut a toile there are certain preparations to make.

1. Check the artist's measurements with the size of your stand, choosing, if possible, one that does not involve too much padding. If the waist is larger in proportion to the bust, for example a 96.5 cm (38 in) bust, 76.2 cm (30 in) waist, 101.16 cm (40 in) hip, choose the 96.5 cm (38 in) bust and pad up the waist and hip. If a 76.2 cm (30 in) waist stand is used the bust size probably 101.6 cm (40 in) would be too big and therefore the back would probably be too broad making it difficult to use.

Likewise if the waist is smaller in proportion to the bust, use a stand with the right waist measurement and pad up the bust.

2. Adjust the height of the stand using the back nape to ground measurement.

3. Always press the fabric before starting to drape the toile.

4. Analyse the design, and try to decide where the seams are and where you are going to fasten the dress.

The placing for the fastening is not always clear, and it will depend on the action of the play or film being performed. For quick changes the opening is usually better at the back, but the design of the costume may look better with a front fastening. If there is a problem it must be discussed at the fitting.

Another consideration is whether or not a dresser is going to be available to dress the artist. Most medieval garments seem to fasten down the centre front and/or at the sides, but they can also fasten down the centre back. Costumes with wide necklines and waists that are confined by a belt can be slipped over the head and kept in place by the belt, if make-up and hair permit.

If reality or costume authenticity is your aim, then the status of the character is an important factor in deciding where to fasten a garment. Characters such as Queens and Ladies are more likely to have back fastenings as they no doubt have servants, whereas the ordinary housewife, young girl or peasant will not and therefore the costume needs a fastening which will allow her to dress herself. Also for the convenience of the artist I have found that, especially on location filming where a dresser might not always be available, artists like front fastenings so as to be able to let themselves out of potentially uncomfortable costumes.

The six patterns in this chapter are: five different ways to cut the fitted dress or kirtle which can be worn under other garments, such as a sideless surcoat or tabard, or the boat shaped neck style of dress, seen in the second half of the 14th century. The sixth sheet has four sleeve patterns on it which cover the tight sleeves used in this book.

PATTERN SHEET 1. This pattern is cut in four pieces, two fronts and two backs with the straight of grain running from shoulder to hem.

When making a toile keep the pins to the edges of the pieces, DO NOT put pins within the body of the pieces or you will distort the shapes.

Pattern Sheet 1.   Cut Through Dress on Straight of Grain

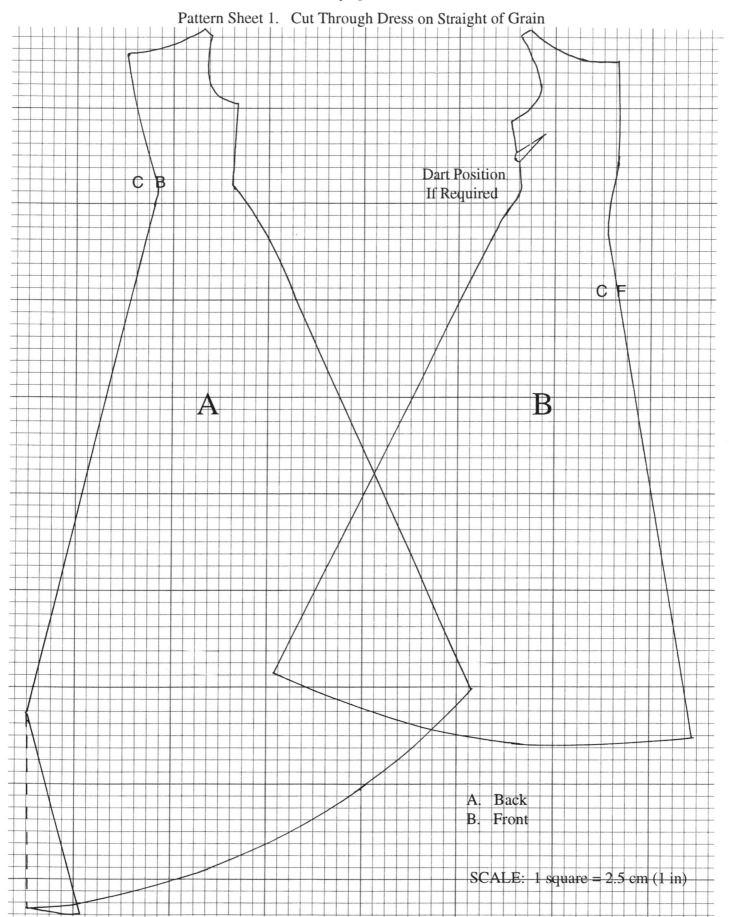

C B

Dart Position
If Required

C F

A

B

A. Back
B. Front

SCALE: 1 square = 2.5 cm (1 in)

1. Pin the fabric on the straight of the grain down the centre front neck and bust area of the stand. Smooth it across from the neck and bust, out to the shoulder and armhole, keeping the grain straight across the stand. Pin the fabric to the shoulder line.

2. Repeat at the back.

3. Starting at the back smooth the fabric down to the waist, angling it so that the centre back is no longer on the straight — the degree to which it will be off the straight will depend on the bust-to-waist ratio. The larger the waist the less it is off the grain.

4. Repeat at the front but lift slightly at the side of the bust, moving the surplus into the armhole to allow for movement. Depending on the ratio of bust to waist and the smoothness required in the finished garment, a small dart or easing will be needed between the underarm and the waist.

The fabric at this stage needs manipulating, quite skilfully, in order to dispose of any surplus material, without using a dart.

5. Pin the shoulders and sides together.

6. Draw the shape of the neck and armhole on to the toile and trim away the surplus fabric. *Trimming away the surplus will release the tension and allow the garment to relax and become easier on the stand or body.* Stand back from the stand and look at the design and the toile, and complete any final adjustment.

The toile is then continued over the hip in a smooth line and continued to the ground. The skirt size of this pattern is the equivalent of about half a circle. It can be made larger or smaller by moving the side and back lines.

The type of fabric used for a fitted dress in four panels, whether it is on the straight or the bias, is very important. It must be pliable so that it will mould to the body (Plate 9, 10, 11.)

Plate 11. Finished back view of toile, showing both straight and bias toiles.

Plate 9. Toile on straight.

Plate 10. Finish toile on straight.

PATTERN SHEET 2. This pattern is cut on the bias and, as can be seen from the pattern, because of the stretch achieved by the bias cut, less shape is needed to make it fit smoothly over the body. It will require 'ease' down the centre front, which is achieved by putting in a row of gathering threads and easing it in. If the fabric is

Pattern Sheet 2. Cut Through Dress on the Bias

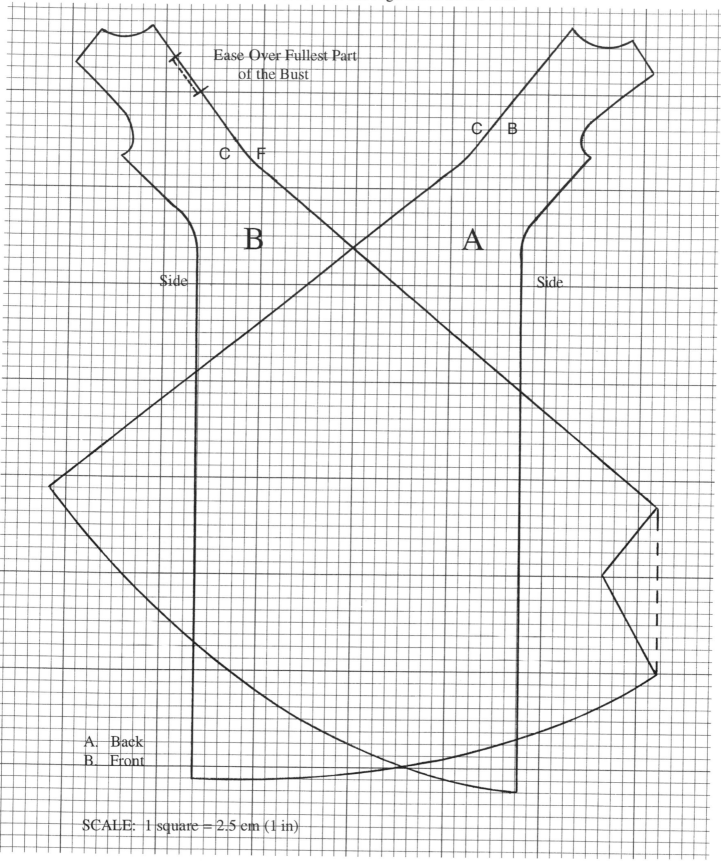

Ease Over Fullest Part
of the Bust

C B

C F

B

A

Side

Side

A. Back
B. Front

SCALE: 1 square = 2.5 cm (1 in)

Plate 12. Toile on Bias showing ease at armhole.

Plate 13. Back view of toile.

Plate 14. Finished Bias toile.

a pure wool, when the seams have been finally stitched together, it can then be pressed with a steam iron or damp cloth to shrink the surplus away. (Plates 11, 12, 13, 14.)

The toile is made in the same way as the first dress but this time start with the bias across from neck to shoulder. Do not pull the fabric down and across as with a straight cut garment, but diagonally along the straight grains.

PATTERN SHEET 3. This pattern was moulded on a princess line in calico. The seam from mid-shoulder to the hem is necessary to get enough shape into a fabric which would be difficult to mould.

Pattern three was used for the Pamina design from the production of *THE MAGIC FLUTE* directed by Peter Sellers for the 1990 Glyndbourne Opera Season. Costumes were designed by Dunya Ramicova. The opera was set in the late 1960's under a Los Angeles freeway, and loosely based on costume of a hippie community. Although this period has nothing to do with Medieval dress, the design for Pamina, sung by the Chinese soprano Ai-Lan Zhu, was cut on a princess line as Pattern 3.

Extra fabric was added into the skirt by flaring out the fabric at the sides front and back seams. Starting at either bust point or shoulder level, and keeping the centres front and back on the straight

Plate 15. Design for the Pamina costume, by Dunya Ramicova, for "The Magic Flute."

Pattern Sheet 3. Cut Through Princess Line Dress

A. Back
B. Side Back
C. Side Front
D. Front

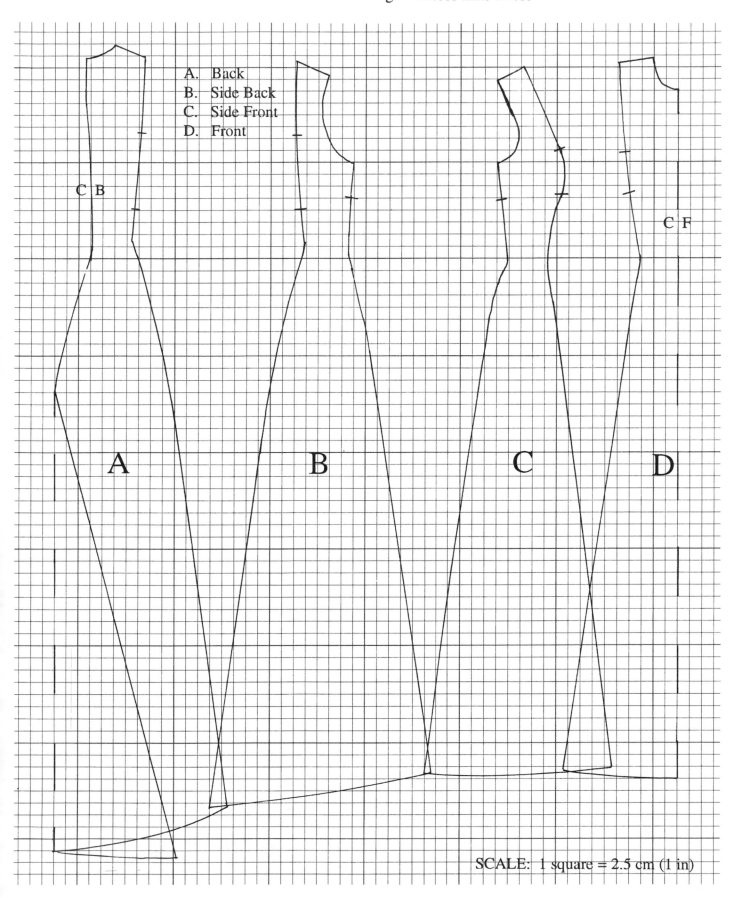

SCALE: 1 square = 2.5 cm (1 in)

of the grain, the side backs and fronts were pivoted round as if cut from a quarter circle.

The body seam of the dress was stitched together as far as the hip, the seam being pressed flat as a box pleat.

The dress was cut and constructed like this so the extra fabric in the skirt did not have to be supported by stitching across on the surface of the dress but by the continuous length of fabric from the start of the flare.

The fabric, a man-made tabby weave, was about 150 cm (60 in.) wide, avoiding the use of wheel pieces. The dress, made by Beryl Horsfield in the Glyndbourne Wardrobe Department, was difficult to make because the sides and centre pieces were not on the same grain, the sides stretching on the centre pieces. I recall them being tacked and allowed to drop about three times to get a perfect hang. All raw seams were pinked so that any finishing would not create a ridge, and the centre front was closed with a nylon 'Optilion'™ zip.

Plate 16. Finished dress made for Pamina in the "Magic Flute", on a stand in the workshop.

The cuffs were finished with wide metal bracelets and the neck by a large necklace. From the auditorium the seams of the dress were not obvious and there was no visible opening. It was worn over a fine licra allover leotard to avoid bra and pantie lines.

PATTERN SHEET 4. This pattern has side panels and a sleeve with a built in square gusset and side panels. I suppose it could be made to cling but I like it best when it is made in jersey or clinging fabric and allowed to glide over the body. (Plate 17 and 18.)

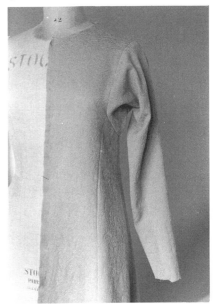

Plate 17. Cut through dress , sleeve with Square Gusset.

Plate 18. The body of the dress should not lift up when the arm is raised. (Plate 4.)

Pattern Sheet 4.   Cut Through Dress with Square Gusset and Cut Through Side Panels

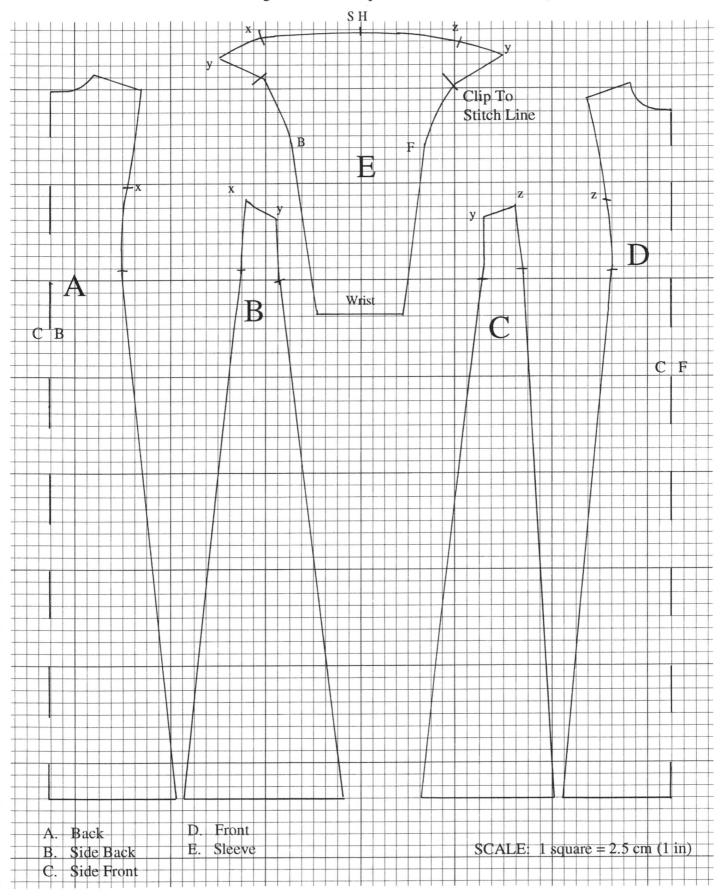

A.   Back

B.   Side Back

C.   Side Front

D.   Front

E.   Sleeve

SCALE: 1 square = 2.5 cm (1 in)

Patterns 2 and 3 are modern interpretations with a set in sleeve and can be made to fit like a second skin. Pattern 1 could be cut with a straight shoulder seam, extending into a T-shape sleeve, and the addition of an underarm gusset. But there would be some wrinkling round the armhole and across the shoulders.

The costumes made from the first four patterns will hang well, and can be made to fit or glide gracefully over the body. They are the type of garment shape that a designer will accept and that an artist will be happy to wear. In the fifth pattern the skirt has far more seams, and depending the type of fabric used, the front and back godets may be difficult to put into the centre of the panels. The pattern will also be difficult to fit, by which I mean, getting all the seams, many of which are on different grains, as well as the fullness of the skirt, to hang well. The fabric to make Pattern 5 needs to be a firm wool, which is not too thick and will not drop or stretch too much.

PATTERN SHEET 5. This pattern is an adaptation from one of the dresses from the famous Greenland grave clothes, said to be mid-thirteenth century. (Plate 19.) The patterns for these garments have been published for many years and can be found in books such as Köhlers "A History of Costume." A more up-to-date

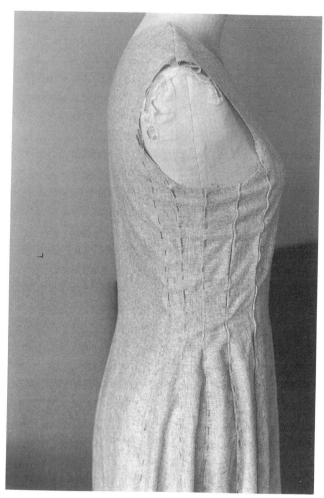

Plate 20. Toile of Greenland Grave Dress.

appraisal with patterns and photographs can be found in 'Bockstensman-nens Draktplagg' by Dr. Margareta Nockert, published in 1985. From the photographs of this particular woman's dress there appears to be no opening, which means the bodice was wide enough to get the head and shoulders through, which would in turn leave the bodice quite loose. To make this baggy bodice comfortable to wear, unless as is suggested by Köhler, it was lined with fur, it was perhaps held in by a belt. The fullness over the hip of the original pattern appears to be low and full and I find it difficult to visualise how it would hang; this, of course, would depend on how soft and malleable the fabric from which it is made would have been when new.

From the armhole of the costumes in the publication by Dr. Nockert, it would seem that many of the garments would have set-in sleeves but

Plate 19. Pattern from the Norse Settlement Herjolfsnes, Greenland of a woman's dress, (after P. Norlund.)

Pattern Sheet 5. Cut Through Dress as Bog Dress

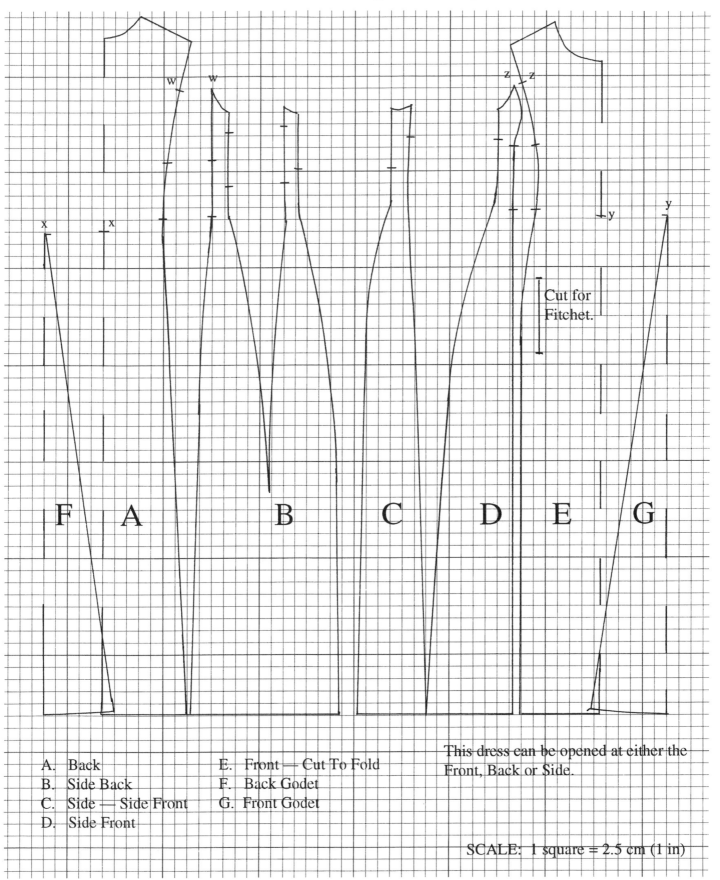

Cut for Fitchet.

F   A   B   C   D   E G

A. Back
B. Side Back
C. Side — Side Front
D. Side Front

E. Front — Cut To Fold
F. Back Godet
G. Front Godet

This dress can be opened at either the Front, Back or Side.

SCALE: 1 square = 2.5 cm (1 in)

only one pattern for this type of sleeve is given. The seam is at the back of the arm and the head is shallow. Some of the dresses have fitchets, (Figure 45) made either in a seam or cut into the body of a panel. The toile was cut in grey flannel which I cut into 51 cm (20 in) wide strips to produce a modern version. (Plate 20) The bodice fits and the hip shaping I have brought into a more natural position for a 40.5 cm (16 in) nape-to-waist back measurement. The dress could be fastened either at the centre front or back or at the side. Sleeve Ca on Pattern 6 or the sleeve on Pattern 4 would look right and could be adapted for this style.

PATTERN SHEET 6. Sleeves A and B have a modern base and a theatrical built in underarm gusset.

Sleeve Ca is cut on the bias with a back seam and a small gusset at the back of the head Cb. This type of gusset can often be seen in the back views of Italian paintings. It can also be cut with a built in underarm gusset (follow dash line) or it can be cut on the straight. This sleeve can be adopted and used as an undersleeve for many of the hanging sleeve patterns described in this book.

The built-in gusset, when cut correctly allows the arm to be raised above the head. The gusset must be cut between 8 or 10 cm (3 or 4 in) deep at the underarm, and quite high at both the front and the back so that when the arm it raised the gusset acts like a hinge. If you are unsure of the depth of the gusset, get the artist to lift the arm at the fitting and either take fabric out or let a little more in from the allowance.

I am afraid that the advent of the T-shirt has meant that both the artists and directors expect the arms to be as mobile as when they are wearing modern clothes. At Glyndebourne we always supplied for rehersal, skirts, and if necessary a calico mock-up of the bodice, which restricted the movement as much as the finished dress.

Sleeves are not always cut as one would ex-

pect, a good example is sleeve Pattern 4D although later in date than our period, it is a sixteenth century bias cut sleeve in the Museum of London collection which has a gore or gusset at the elbow to give the sleeve shape, rather than the later two piece or darted sleeve (Figure 31.)

Figure 31. An early 16th century bias cut sleeve which has a gore or gusset at the elbow.

Pattern Sheet 6.   Four Sleeve Patterns

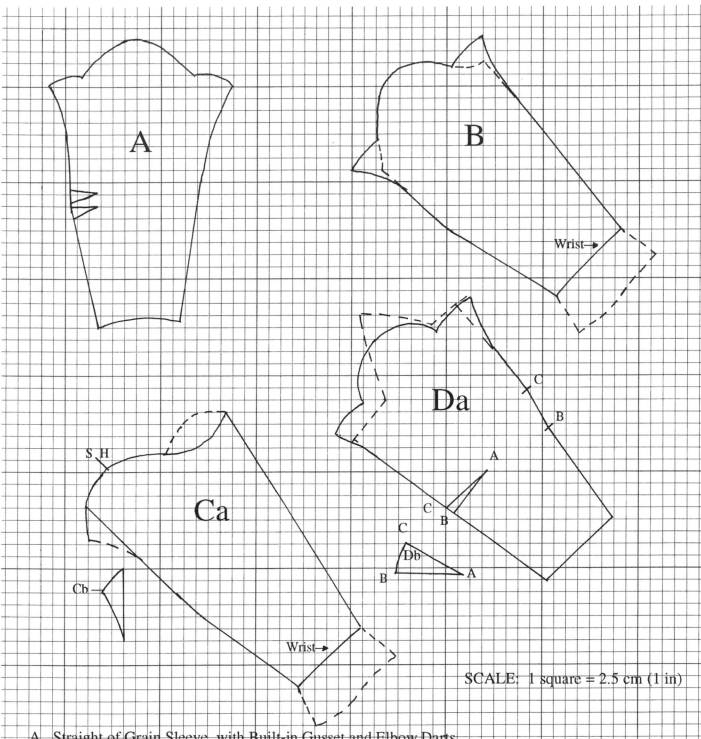

SCALE: 1 square = 2.5 cm (1 in)

A. Straight of Grain Sleeve, with Built-in Gusset and Elbow Darts.
B. Bias Sleeve. - - - - Denotes Cuff and Sleeve Without Gusset
C. a. Bias Sleeve with Back Seam. - - - - Denotes Built-in Underarm Gusset and Cuff.
      b. Gusset.
D. a. Museum of London, 16th Century Bias Sleeve, with
      b. Elbow Gusset.

Photo © Ira Norwinski

Plate 21. Many operas in a Repertory theatre such as Glyndebourne are re-mounted over the life span of the production. The dress, being adjusted in the photographs, worn in Act II of "Così fan Tutte" by Mozart, was made new for Isobel Buchanan who sang Dorabella for the 1987 re-mount of the Sir Peter Halls 1978 production, which was designed by John Bury. My assistant, Sandra Baybutt, is easing in the piping cord, from the back, which finishes the neckline of the dress, to tighten and make the neckline fit snugly to the figure. (Left to Right.) Jean Hunnisett, Isobel Buchanan and Jean's assistant, Sandra.

6. Making a basic dress

My motto in costume making is — "it just depends". The final success depends on the design, and the suitability of the fabric for that design, the imagination of the cutter, the skill of the maker, the trimming, decoration and many other things. The medieval period is susceptible to all of these problems. If the fabric is too solid it won't drape. If the weave is too loose it will drop too much and become a string of a garment. Many man-made fabrics or stiff silks do not mould well and are apt to poke in all the wrong places. There is also a problem in how the lining and the skirt fabric of a large full skirt, especially when the dress is picked up, is to be held together.

Having said all that, medieval costume is relatively easy to put together; the difficulty lies in the large size of the pattern pieces. From a purely theatrical point of view, the fewer seams there are the better. Unless great care and skill is used, the sewing machine is apt to tighten up the seams making them pucker, whereas with a hand-sewn seam, the medieval seamstress would be able to judge the tension of the thread through her fingers. On stage or screen nothing looks worse than a spider's web of unnecessary seams especially if they are badly stitched.

Costumes made with large pattern pieces are difficult to mount successfully, unless it is known that both top fabric and mounting will drop at the same rate. If the dress is cut through and the lining is not caught to the dress hem, it is far better to drop a lining in from the shoulder. But if the dress has a waist or hip seam, drop the lining in from that seam and mount the bodice on to a suitable fabric. For bodices I use cotton drill for heavy fabrics and a lighter weight cotton for lightweight fabrics or sleeve linings. The choice will depend on the style and the fabric of the dress.

To Make a Toile into a Pattern

The technique for making-up a successful dress with large pattern pieces seems time consuming, but most of the individual operations take very little time.

Strengthen all the markings made on the toile, and transfer the shape on to pattern paper, taking care to mark in the grain lines and balance marks. Or, the toile itself can be used as a pattern. I usually cut off all the allowances on the toile before using it as a pattern or putting it on to paper.

The secret for making a successful dress is giving the large pieces sufficient time to hang.

Long seams must be put together with great care; the machine stitching must not hold them too tightly. Likewise, if the seams are straight to flare, the flare side must be stretched just enough so that it neither swags on, nor pulls up the straight edge.

Use the following technique to make up costumes with large pattern pieces.

1. Lay the pattern onto the fabric and cut, clip the selvedges to release the edge threads as you proceed. Pin the pieces from the shoulders, or if the bodice section is too slender to bear the weight of the skirt — as with the surcoat — from the hip and pin them on to a wall, or suspend on tapes from a coat hanger, and leave overnight.

2. Pin or tack the seams and hang again or alternatively and better, leave on a dress stand to mould into the shape of a body.

3. After adjusting any seams that have dropped — and there will be some depending on the type of fabric — machine them together and press.

Mounting and Making the Bodice and Sleeves

If the bodice is not cut in one with the skirt, it may need to be mounted on to an interlining. When needed I use a good quality drill or firm sheeting. For tight sleeves I try to use a slippery fabric such as a light-weight cotton sateen, or a man-made lining fabric. The advantage of cotton is that it is more absorbent than man made, but a slippery fabric will allow the arm to slide into the sleeve more easily. The design of the costume and the type of material will dictate whether or not a mounting is necessary.

Mounting must be done very carefully and all the layers must be pressed flat with no creases. All the pieces should be treated in the same way.

Any bones that are needed to stiffen the bodice are applied to the outside of the mounting fabric — away from the body. (See Sewing Techniques — Rigilene.)

1. Trace the pattern on to the twill side of the drill and the boning pattern on to the reverse.
2. Bone each pattern piece and then press the pieces to take the curve out of the boning.
3. Lay the top fabric face down on the table and smooth out the creases.

Some thin fabrics or a bodice which is boned will need a layer of thin domette, or sheeting between the top and mounting fabrics to create a thicker look, or to stop the pattern of the boning from showing through the fabric. Domette is rarely used in sleeves.

4. If you are using domette lay that on to the fabric and smooth.
5. Next lay the mounting piece, boned side down, onto the domette, so that you can see the marks of the seam allowance. Pin the fabrics together from the lining side, pinning into the seam allowance only. (This avoids pin holes in the top fabric).
6. Turn the piece over to the right side and smooth from top to bottom and side to side, to make sure there is no surplus fabric or wrinkles.
7. Turn back again to the lining side and flat tack the layers together.
8. Tack the bodice pieces together by hand or on a large machine stitch. (See Flat tack.)
9. Continue to make up the bodice by joining all the bodice seams together matching the balance marks.
10. When making up sleeves with a built in gusset, the corners must be reinforced and clipped as far as the machine line. The centre of the gusset should match the natural underarm seam position. The gusset should not make the sleeve head larger unless the seam has been splayed out.

The technique of splaying the sleeve seam is useful when cutting very tight sleeves, but remember to also splay the top of the under arm seam of the bodice by the same amount so that the two will fit together.

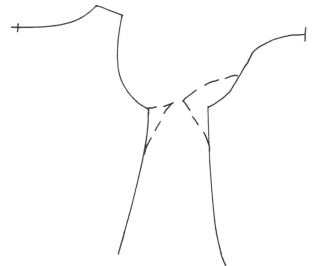

Figure 32. The sleeve and Bodice seam splayed when making a tight bodice and sleeve. The sleeve also has a built in gusset.

11. Tack the sleeves into the bodice and then if the waist is high tack the bodice on to the skirt.

FIRST FITTING. (See Fitting chapter.)

12. After the fitting do any alterations, machine and finish the seams and put in the placket where required.
13. Finish the sleeves and tack them into the armholes.

14. If the dress has a loose lining, catch it to the shoulder seam and the side seams as far as the waist.

If the skirt is cut independently from the bodice, machine the lining and the skirt together at the waist before joining it to the bodice.

15. Prepare the hem — the shape of which has been marked at the fitting on one side only. To transfer the line to the other half, fold the skirt in half from the centres front and back. Pin the waist and balance marks together, arrange the two sides flat, one on top of the other, taking care to match the grain lines of the fabric. Small variations in the shape of the line can be straightened out but trust your original fitting marks for the general sweep of a large circular hem. Treat the lining — if there is one — in the same way.

16. Tack up the hem.

WATCH POINTS

Where the fabric falls on the bias of a large circular piece of fabric it will dropped much more at that point than at any other. This will make it appear shorter when it is laid out on the flat, but when it is allowed to fall under its own weight it will be the right length.

If the artist has a large hip this will lift the fabric in places, making it appear long when on the flat.

If the fabric is a very fine one such as chiffon — beware — trim the hem a small amount all the way round, check it all the time to see that it is not sticking to the floor. As chiffon gets shorter and looses the weight at hem level, it can suddenly becomes too short.

I saw this happen many years ago with a dress for Juliet. The skirt was made in three layers of chiffon, the cutter kept trimming the length away, when all at once it was about 5 cm (2 in) off the ground. The weight of the fabric sticking to the ground must have kept it long, as soon as it lost that weight it became too short. Each skirt was made from about eight yards of chiffon, all three

skirts had to be rebought and made again. A very expensive mistake.

SECOND FITTING

At the second fitting check the fit of the sleeve in the armhole, the waist, and hem and discuss any decoration still to be applied. Take samples to the fitting.

After the fitting, machine in the sleeves, finish the waist, hem and any other jobs still outstanding.

HEMS

Hems can be finished in five ways.

1. For a simple hem on a garment which is longer than floor length and made with a loose lining — overlock or zig-zag to finish the edge, then turn up once about 5 mm ($1/4$ in) on the machine. Treat the lining in the same way.

2. Hems can be bagged out, but this is a very unreliable way of turning a long curved hem, and fraught with problems.

3. If it is felt necessary to turn more than between 5 mm–1 cm ($1/4$ in to $3/4$ in) as above, treat as for a modern hem. This again can be fraught with problems for, if the hem is on a curve, the top edge will have to be eased in.

4. If a deeper hem is required it can be faced, onto either the wrong side for a plain hem, or the right side and used as contrasting border. The facing must be cut on the same grain as the dress hem, or as a bias strip if the curve is not too great.

If the skirt is to be worn turned back showing a contrasting colour, the method below is by far the best.

5. This method was used in the nineteenth century for putting linings on to court trains, and is still used today for putting together ceremonial robes such as those used for the Order of the Garter. The effect of this method can be seen as a fine cream line visible all round the edge of the navy blue velvet Garter robes, in the paintings at Windsor Castle. Also when the Garter proces-

sion takes place in June at Windsor, look carefully at the television transmissions or in photographs in the press.

The lining must be cut to the same shape as the garment, so that the grains of both fabrics will hang together and are the same circumference. Put them together taking all the precautions described above so that both will have dropped as far as possible.

METHOD 5 (Figure 33.)

a. Machine or hand prick a piping cord into the fold of the hem of the lining, and trim away the surplus fabric to 2 cm (^{3}/4 in).

b. Diagonal tack the two layers of the garment together at the centres, front and back, and all the seams, and probably between the seams as well, stopping about 15 cm (6 in) from the hem line.

c. Pin the two layers together round the bottom, and check from both the outside and the inside that they are lying together smoothly.

d. Trim the top layer so that it is 2 cm (^{3}/4 in) longer than the lining, then turn it up and tack or pin the two together. Let it hang overnight to make sure neither side is dropping or pulling the other out of shape.

e. Turn in the bottom edge of the top fabric and fell it on to the machine line that is holding in the piping.

f. Press lightly so as not to show the impression of the turnings.

The result from the right side should be a good clean edge, with the fine line of the contrasting lining showing. If either fabric drops it is very easy to rectify the problem. If lead weight is needed round the hem or at the back, whip it on to the lining just above the piping cord before the top fabric is felled down. The top fabric can be machined onto the lining but this makes the hem hard and leaves you with two rows of machine stitching on the lining side.

If there are any doubts about the final length of a costume, tack up the hem and wait until after the first dress rehearsal before finishing it.

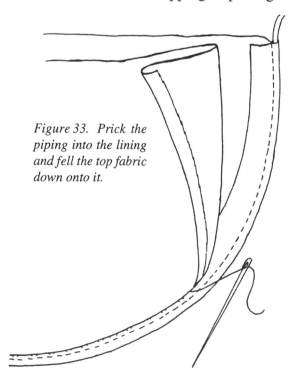

Figure 33. Prick the piping into the lining and fell the top fabric down onto it.

Plate 22. Annette Crosby as Queen Victoria in the 1970's television series, "Edward VII." She is wearing Garter Robes. Across the hem, at ground level, on her left-hand side can be seen the finished edge — the fine white piping against the deep blue velvet — and on the same side, the corner of the robe shows the inside finish, using Hems method 5.

52

7. THE FITTING

After measuring the artist 'the fitting' is one of the most important parts of making a costume. It is the time when, if you are positive in both your technique and opinions and the fitting is good, it will boost not only your own confidence as a cutter and maker but that of both the designer and the artist, in your ability.

Make sure the costume is ready for the fitting. If you have to travel — be on time. Make a check list of all the things you need. In the fitting room put the design on the wall, and if you have a choice, make sure the mirror is clean and well positioned.

If the production is new, besides yourself and the Artist, there will be the Designer and a Wardrobe Supervisor or Buyer. For an important artist there may be the Wardrobe Manager and the Director of the show, especially if he is worried about what his star is going to look like. Try to be as efficient as possible, and keep a check-list of important points you must look for during the fitting.

Try to make your artist feel at ease, he or she may feel very vulnerable. Think how you would feel standing with very few clothes on, in a room full of people you probably do not know very well, and who are probably discussing your appearance as if you are not there.

Before the fitting, check over the measurements of the costume (bust - waist - hips - nape to waist back and waist to ground) to make sure they are correct. It always surprises me how often the waist measurement for instance has not been checked. In the process of putting a costume together, a waist band may tighten up, or enough care may not have been taken when measuring off the length of petersham or webbing for the waist band.

It is also helpful to have a temporary hook and bar on the waistband. Pinning a tight waistband together can be difficult, and the pin dangerous for the artist.

I had a prestigious fitting for a leading lady for a film that took four hours. All the costumes for the film had to be fitted that day, as she was flying off to some other location and I did not see her again until we met on the set with the finished clothes some three months later. I have also been to a fitting when an equally important artist was two hours late and then expected to fit four costumes for a play in half an hour. However, if the groundwork in cutting and care in getting the costume ready for a such fitting has been done properly, all should be well.

If possible, take an assistant with you, especially for long fittings. The job of the assistant is to take good notes, not only of what is decided about a hem length or a piece of decoration, but also to record the discarded ideas. Designers sometimes come back to old ideas or even dispute what they have said. The assistant can clear away fitted costumes, and keep track of bits of trimmings, braid etc., that may have been introduced during the fitting. A good assistant is worth her weight in gold, and a very good partnership can be built up at fittings, each knowing what her job is and doing it efficiently and without fuss. If the cutter is not the maker, as in my time at Glyndebourne, it makes the job of a maker in a workroom, more interesting, and helps her to understand the problems when large alterations are made to the original cut or design if she can see the costume on the artist.

The job of the fitter is to make sure all the basic areas are correct, such as — are there any unwanted wrinkles — is the waist comfortable — is the neck low enough; very important when working with singers — does the sleeve fit into the armhole well — is the hem level? At the same time, other people in the room are usually making 'helpful' suggestions, such as "why can't the skirt be six inches longer than the design" when you know that because the dress has been designed at that length and therefore cut with that in mind, there is not enough fabric to make it three inches longer never mind six.

The order in which the fitter works is important, if a certain routine is followed then nothing gets forgotten.

WATCH POINTS

Always fit one side of a garment only, unless there is some reason such as a discrepancy from one side of the body to the other, such as a dropped shoulder. It is better to put padding into the garment to compensate, than have an uneven fit.

When you come to do the alterations, if you have only fitted one side, any pins on the second side can be ignored, unless you have noted a problem

It is very easy to forget when concentrating on fitting the side of a costume, that you may be pulling the centres front and back off the straight.

GENERAL COSTUME FITTING
(Fit one side only)
1. Put on the chemise or shift if there is one.
2. Put on the corset, or with the period we are dealing with, in this book, probably a tight underdress — the Kirtle (see Kirtle drawings No 53 -4 -5.)

Before tightening the lacing or fastening, make sure that if there is a separate chemise that it is pulled down and that the neckline is in the correct position. If possible fit the kirtle at this point.

3. Make sure that the waist, neck and armholes fits snugly. If necessary clip the allowance at the neck and the armholes to release the tension
4. Put on the next layer, in this period it could be a Sideless Surcoat or a Houppelande. Make sure that it is sitting properly on the shoulders before starting the fitting.
5. Do any major alterations first, such as re-balancing the shoulders to get rid of any pulling or droop.
6. Check that the waist and hip positions are correct and alter accordingly.
7. Check the flat tacking lines round the neck and armhole are correct. If they are wrong, draw a new line with chalk, a pencil, or with a line of pins.
8. When everything is correct, clip the allowance round the neck and armholes — on one side only — to just short of the finished line, then turn in the allowance and pin it flat. This should take the tension and wrinkle from these areas and make the bodice lie flat. The shoulders may now need slight adjustments.
9. Mark the underdress neckline with chalk, either to come above or be the same as the top neckline. Use either chalk marks or safty pins as balance marks so that after the fitting you know where the two necklines fitted together.
10. Mark the hem line.
11. Adjust any other points considered necessary.

After the top garment has been fitted and approved, take it off, making sure the pins are well into the fabric. Also make sure that the garment goes easily over the head. If not discuss where it should be fastened.

The underdress may now need further adjustments. When a garment is worn for only a short

Plate 23. (Above.) Left to right. Jean Hunnisett, her assistant Rossie, Felicity Lott, and Tony Ledell. Ms. Lott is being fitted for her costumes for the opera, 'Capricio' by Richard Strauss. (Note the image in the side mirror.)

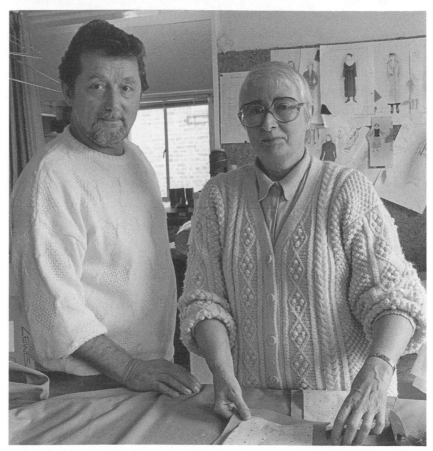

Plate 24. (Right.) Tony Ledell and Jean Hunnisett, in Jean's cutting room.

time, especially when worn under another, it gets warm and the fabric relaxes. If the fit is good it will have taken the shape of the artists body and need only minor adjustments. If not it will look a wreck and need refitting.

If for some reason, such as the complete costume needs to be seen to get an overall impression before it is fitted. Run your eyes over it, clipping the neck and armholes making sure you are not strangling your artist.

TO FIT THE SURCOAT

1. Make sure the plakard is the right length and width.

Apart from the usual points, such as necklines etc. check the following points.

2. For a sway back; if the back drops the artist probably has a hollow or sway back. This is quite common in dancers. Pick up the back at the shoulder and lift until it is level with the front.

3. For round shoulders — the reverse of a sway back — either drop the back, which could make the back neck too low or lift the front. If the front is lifted make sure that the bust shaping, if any, does not get out of place.

4. Check that the surcoat grips the hip, if extra fabric has been put into the side when cutting to create a pleat as with Queen Jeanne (Surcoat and Cloaks Figure 85.) which will give more leeway when fitting, adjust the size of the pleat.

FITTING THE UNDERDRESS OR KIRTLE

If the bust is to be flattened by the underdress it must be made of a firm fabric, but if it is too thin it must be mounted onto a firm drill.

If possible no bra should be worn so that the breast will take on a rounded shape formed by the underdress. This will make it easier to make a four piece bodice with no darts, fit.

1. Check that the hipline is in the correct place or if there is no hip seam, where the belt should fit.

2. The back will be relatively easy to fit without wrinkles if the bodice is waist length.

However, at the front if there is too much fullness under the arm creating wrinkles, the surplus must be passed across at both the top and the bottom of the bodice into the centre front seam which will then curve in at both ends. (see Kirtle pattern 12)

3. To do this rip the shoulder seam and move any surplus fullness across towards the centre front neck — usually about 1cm (^{1}/2 in). Leaving a certain amount of ease at the side of the bust and around the armhole. Re-pin the shoulder and front seams.

4. Now repeat this operation on the lower part of the bodice, ripping the side seam and moving the surplus down and across to the centre front waist, again re-pinning the seams.

5. Re-mark the armhole, neckline and bottom of the bodice.

This is not an easy operation but practice on a stand moving the fullness from an underarm dart around a bodice will help the understanding of the technique.

Remember only do this operation on one side of the bodice, keeping it pinned together at the centre front across the fullest part of the bust.

PART TWO:

Patterns and Detail

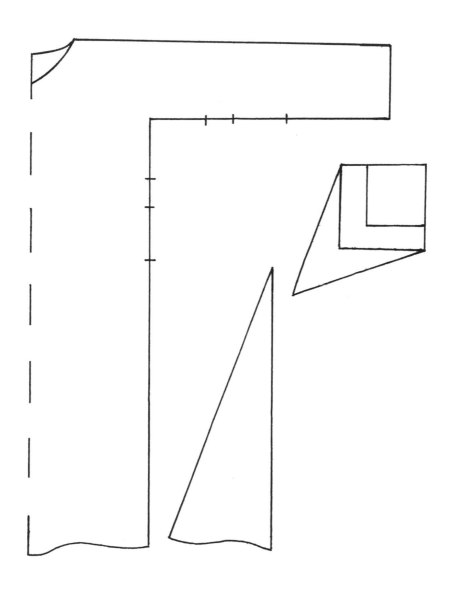

8. MIDDLE AGES — 1400 A.D.

The developement of costume from the Early Christian T-shaped Dalmatic of the 4th century, which in turn had developed from Roman dress, comes down to us through some of the garments worn by the clergy and the monastic orders. Likewise the influence of the Byzantine Empire with its glowing colours, beautiful fabrics and elaborately decorated costumes, the remnants of which can still be seen in the dress of the Orthodox churches. These organizations grew to dominate most of Europe, and have left us a legacy of the robes we see in our churches today.

The barbarian invasions across feudal Europe during the 9th and 10th century from Nordic and Eastern lands, affected the lives of most of its people and must have influenced and inhibited the way in which they dressed.

In the 11th and 12th Centuries, the Crusades brought to the West a greater awareness of the culture of the East, introducing silks and fine gauzes from the Levant, China and India, into European dress.

In the 13th century, wool was exported from England and Spain to Flemish cities such Bruges and Ghent where it was woven into cloth and exported back into England as well as to Southern Europe. Today, when so many different types of goods are exported all over the world, it must be remembered that it was the export and import of wool and the cloth made from it that created much of the wealth of the time. The money generated by the merchants trading between the Mediterranean and Northern Europe built up thriving cities and towns, creating a whole new middle class, which in turn influenced the manner in which people dressed.

In the second and third quarters of the Twelfth Century the main garments worn by women became tight fitting as if made in a knitted or stretchy fabric or perhaps cut on the bias. The close fitting sleeves often ended in a pendulous cuff, starting about 15 cm (6 in) above the wrist, and called by Joseph Strutt in his "Dress and Habits of the People of England" a Pocketing sleeve (Figure 34.)

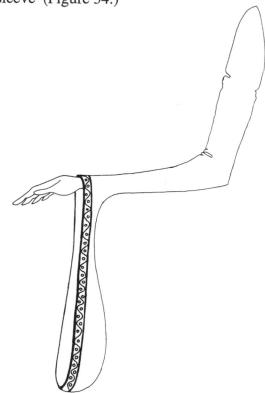

Figure 34. Pocketing sleeve.

Two examples of this fashion, which was probably worn only by upperclass women, are: first, an elaborate version dated approximately 1150, of a biblical Queen from the sculptures at Chartres Cathedral, (Figure 35); and second, dated 1160-70, according to Claire Donovan in a joint British Library/Winchester Cathedral Publication about THE WINCHESTER BIBLE, the arm. It varies in size, as the three illustrations, one woman and two men, from a 13th century English Apocalypse (Figure 37, 38, 39) shows. The woman is wearing a plain dolman sleeved gown, but the first man's sleeve is much more exaggerated, with extra fullness cut into the under-arm. Under the low neck and calf length skirt of his Super-tunic, can be seen his Tunic. Both versions of this sleeve are tight from wrist to elbow, and both garments are controlled by the belt. The second man wears an unbelted version of a garment with a dolman sleeve, which is wide at the end, and he wears a mantle over his Super-tunic. The underarm fullness at this period can be achieved by putting a very large gusset into the under arm of the garment. Cutting the tunic with a dolman shaped body does not create sufficient bulk under the arm to equate with the illustrations.

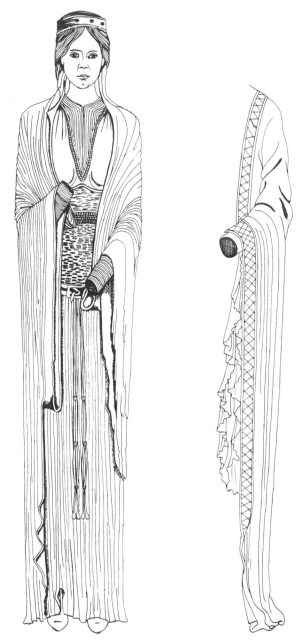

Figure 35. 1150. *Biblical Queen from the Sculptures at Chartres Cathedral.*

character of Wisdom (Figure 36), is one of the unfinished illuminations.

By the 13th Century the T-shaped Gown, now called a Kirtle, was back in fashion, but instead of being cut straight as in earlier times, it is now cut on an 'A' line shape which became wider and much longer than in earlier periods. The gown is controlled by pouching it over a belt. The sleeve also changes to a batwing or dolman shape which hangs in drapes under the

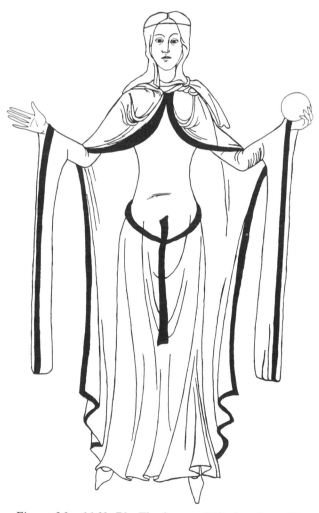

Figure 36. 1160–70. *The figure of Wisdom from 'The Winchester Bible.'*

The drawing of 1260 taken from a French manuscript called 'The Book of Old Testament Illustrations' (Figure 40) shows the dress sliding loosely over the body and widening out at the hip into a very long full skirt. The gown is controlled by pulling some of the length into a pouch through a girdle which is worn low on the waist. The under arm gusset is now smaller making the sleeve appear more slender than before.

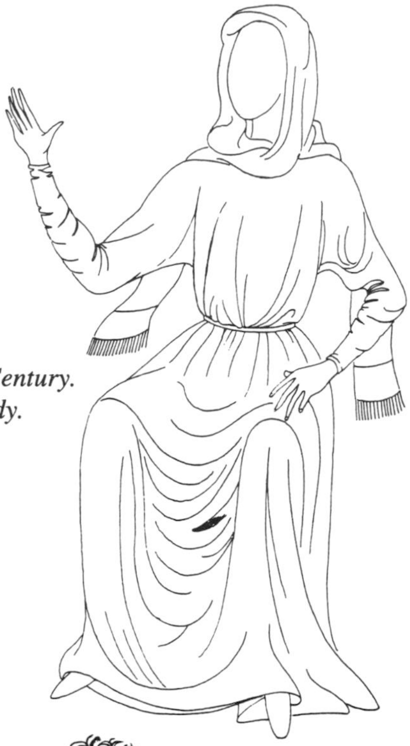

Figure 37.
English , 13th Century.
Apocalypse, Lady.

Figure 39.   English, 13th Century. Apocalypse, Man— The second man, with sleeves wide at the wrists.

Figure 38.   English, 13th Century.   Apocalypse, Man.
The first man with exaggerated underarm fullness

By the beginning of the 14th century the dress of both men and women is still very similar. What we see today is mainly a monk's eye view of what was happening in medieval Europe, so that the account of women's dress is particularly limited.

The Luttrell Psalter of 1340 is a mine of information on the costume, of both men and women and of all classes of people. The orange kirtle worn by Lady Luttrell (Figure 41) under her surcoat which is in blue and gold decorated with armorial bearings, is tighter fitting than those of the late 13th Century. Another lady (Figure 42) in the same manuscript wears a loose gown or Cote Hardie over her kirtle, the sleeve being tight to the elbow, and cut with grown on lappets, which are lined with fur. The underdress has tight sleeves to the wrist and both garments now have a neck line which is a daring boat shape.

Figure 40. 1260.
From 'The Book of Old
Testament Illustrations.'

Figure 41. (Below.) 1340. From the Luttrell Psalter. Orange Kirtle, worn by Lady Luttrell, under a blue and gold decorated Surcoat.

Figure 42. (Above.) 1340. A Lady from the Luttrell Psalter. She is wearing a Cote Hardie, with a daring boat shaped neckline, over a Kirtle.

One of my favourite early 14th century ladies, is this back view, also from the Luttrell Psalter, (Figure 43) which shows the small circular lappets at the end of elbow length sleeves, and also the fullness of the skirt swinging from the high hip.

The Luttrell Psalter also shows good examples of the peasant dress of its date. The clothes of working peoples throughout this period do not change a great deal.

In this frontview from Strutt (Figure 44) of a long loose over dress, again the elbow length sleeves have small lappets. The skirt of the underdress has an interesting hem which appears to be stitched or pinned up in pockets.

By the end of the third quarter of the 14th century the merchants classes wore clothes made in better fabrics, and of a more tailored style, not just garments to keep themselves warm. Drawings of two nearly identical dresses; the first a weeper, dated 1377, from the tomb of Edward the III in Westminster Abbey (Figure 45), shows a dress with a boat neck which fits closely to the figure as far as the low hip, and is fastened down the front by large buttons. From the hip it widens out into a skirt which falls, as if cut from flared panels or segments of a circle. The slits in the skirt are known as fitchets; the hands could slide through to a purse slung from a belt round the kirtle underneat (see Cloaks and Surcoats Figure 86.) According to Cunnington's "Handbook of English Medieval Costume", fitchets first appeared in *c.* 1250. The tight sleeve which ends just above the elbow is finished with a band from which hang long narrow tippets. The sleeves of the kirtle reach to the base of the thumb.

The second dress, which is very similar, is from a brass in Chrishall, Essex of Joan de la Pole dated 1380 (Figure 46.) The line of the dress is the same, but it has smaller

Figure 43. 1340. Rear view, depictingcircular lappets at the end of elbow length sleeves from the Lutrell Psalter.

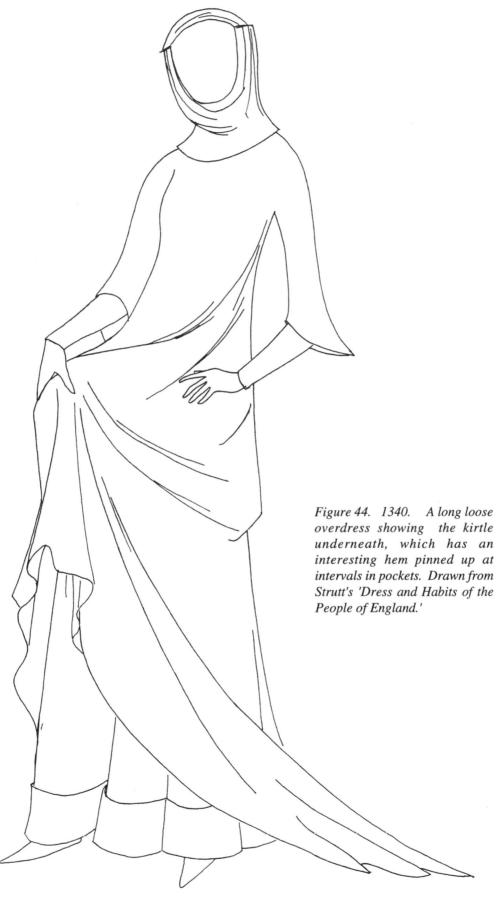

Figure 44. 1340. A long loose overdress showing the kirtle underneath, which has an interesting hem pinned up at intervals in pockets. Drawn from Strutt's 'Dress and Habits of the People of England.'

Figure 45. 1377. A weeper, from the Tomb of Edward III in Westminster Abbey.

Figure 46. 1380. Joan de la Pole, from a brass in Chrishall, Essex.

buttons down the front and the sleeves are buttoned from the knuckles to above the elbow, finishing just under the tippet band, but there are no fitchets in the skirt.

In the Museum of London series on 'Finds from Excavations in London' number 4 'Textile and Clothing'; the research has shown that buttons were in practical use in northern Europe in the first half of the 13th century and that by the early years of the 14th they were being used as a fashion feature. The photograph is of a cuff from the museum collection (Plate 25) and shows the closeness of the buttons and holes, as well as the skill of the dressmaker. The buttonhole edge is faced with silk (Figure 47) through which the

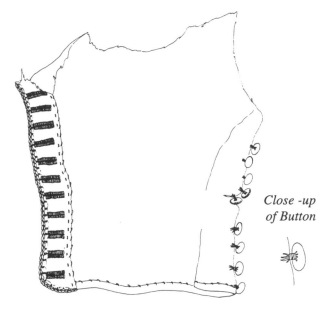

Close-up of Button

Figure 47.   Drawing of the inside of the Museum of London Cuff, showing Silk Facing, Turnings and Buttons.

Plate 25.   A cuff from a deposit dating to the first quarter of the 14th Century. Museum of London.

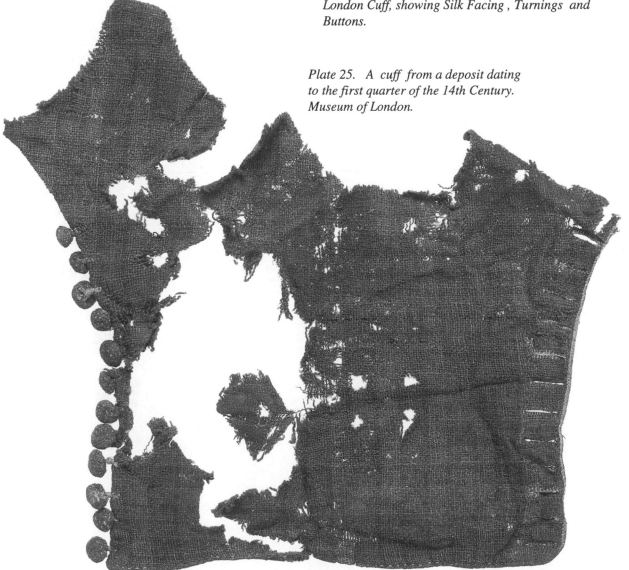

buttonholes are worked, and the edge of the cuff, which is a single layer of fabric is finished with a tablet-woven edge. This is a feature seen on many dresses to the end of the century.

The next drawing, from a memorial brass, shows a dress which, like Lady Luttrell's surcoat, is decorated with armorial bearings, it is of Lady Harsick (Figure 48) and is dated 1384. It appears from the quarterings to be cut in at least four panels, with a centre front seam. These sleeves also have buttons which reach to the bend at the elbow, but some illustrations show buttons reaching much further up the arm. It is worn with a half circular cloak, the cord of which she is holding between her finger and thumb, a practice which goes back to the 13th century.

The last dress in this series shows an example from an enamel of 1380. (Figure 49) It is similar to those above, but it is cut so that the waist appears higher, anticipating the waistline seen in the early Houppelande styles. Note the sleeves of the overdress which are turned back above the elbow showing clearly the buttonholes and the kirtle sleeves underneath.

There are many plays and operas set in this period, Shakespeare's "King John" is set in the beginning of the 13th Century and "Richard II" at the end of the 14th, and Marlowe's "Edward II" at the beginning of the same century. Rossini's "William Tell", is set in 13th century Switzerland and "Le Compte Ory" at the time of the crusades. Of Wagner's operas "Parsifal" is set at the end of the 12th and "Tannhäuser" in the early 13th. Films and television use this period for series such as "Robin Hood". B.B.C. Television produced a series called the "The Devil's Crown", designed by John Bloomfield. I dressed Queens Beringaria, Matilda and Eleanor of Aquitaine. "Murder in the Cathedral" by T.S. Eliot, and "The Lark and Becket" by Jean Anouilh are perennials of theatre companies.

Dating from the early 14th century are the

Figure 48. 1384. Lady Hersick from a memorial brass.

68

Medieval Mystery Plays of cities such as Chester and York which were performed by the guilds. Parts of these cycles are still performed today.

Fabrics suitable for the early part of the period are wools, noiles and heavy silk with both a smooth or textured finish. For the later fitted styles, a fabric which will mould to the body without too many seams would be better. For costumes of the 14th century, velvet and velveteen can be used. From the Wardrobe accounts of Edward II, velvet was purchased in 1320. Fur also becomes very popular, linings of fur appear in cloaks and surcoats one suspects not only to keep the wearer warm but to show the depth of the owner's pocket.

Although I do not deal specifically with men's costume, the same technique for cutting and making womens clothes can be used for both. Most men's costumes need to be more strongly made than the women's and the fabric requires more body. If they are to be mounted something firm will be needed.

Set-in sleeves are not used during most of this period, but this does not mean that the garment

Figure 49. 1380. Lady from an enamel.

needs to be shapeless. Fullness or shaping can be added to T-shaped garments, by inserting a gore or godet where it is required to give more width or for easier movement. The basic T-shaped sleeve with an under arm gusset or even just a split, although it will not fit without wrinkles round the armhole, will look more authentic than a set-in sleeve. It is not known when the set in sleeve made its first appearance, but it seems unlikely that it was much before the middle of the 14th century. The tightness of the body, and the absence of wrinkles round the armholes displayed in much of the visual source material, suggests that it was likely that a sleeve with a head had been developed by the end of the century.

WATCH POINTS

If a costume is made up of an over dress and an under dress, only the sleeves and lower part of the under dress will show. If the fabric is expensive or is printed, mount only those parts which show, onto a plain base made in an inexpensive cloth.

When one garment is worn over another, mount the over dress on to a fine slippy lining, which will help both garments to move independently.

Clothes that are put on over the head, or have a very limited opening, are not practical for the theatre. If 'a way in' has to be found to avoid problems with make-up and hair, try to make the fastening as unobtrusive as possible, such as under a piece of decoration or in the shoulder seam. An opening can be made at the back if there is a seam, or a cloak or drape is to be worn over the gown.

Making a costume for this period, apart from mounting the fabric where necessary, can be achieved by modern methods of dressmaking, as described in Sewing Techniques and Making a Basic Dress in Part I.

I am afraid that I am probably not going to solve the historical problems of cutting Medieval dress in this book, however, with the amount of time I have spent studying the references, I feel that I have trained my eyes to sort out the various layers of the garments in the illustrations, and I hope that I have placed the right interpretation on them.

CONTROL

Unfortunately not all artists are the ideal shape to wear some of the long uncluttered lines of this period. If it is felt that to achieve the right shape or that the shape of the artist needs more control, a leotard or if necessary an all over leotard, with legs and sleeves made in Lycra, can be used. They can usually be bought from dance or sports shops. If firmer control is needed, a corselet type of foundation can usually be bought from lingerie departments of large stores, but the breast shape, which can usually be altered quite easily, must look rounded and natural. If alteration is needed, to make the foundation the correct shape, buy one size larger than required and there will be enough fabric in it to change the shape.

Plain Lycra is fairly easy to buy, but the heavier weights, textured types, and corsetry fabrics and the soft edgeing elastics needed to make firm foundations are more difficult to obtain, except in wholesale houses who are often reluctant to sell in small quantities.

I do not intend to give patterns for this type of garment as using stretch fabrics is a specialized craft.

PATTERNS FOR COSTUMES IN THIS CHAPTER

Pattern Sheet 7. Basic T-Shapes show how to manipulate a T-shaped garment, and how the shape of the garment can be changed by using various sizes and shapes of gussets, into either square or diamond shaped armholes. The measurement of the pattern round the bust is 102 cm (40 in) and the gusset will add width to that measurement.

Pattern Sheet 7.   Two Basic 'T-Shaped' Garments with Alternative Gussets

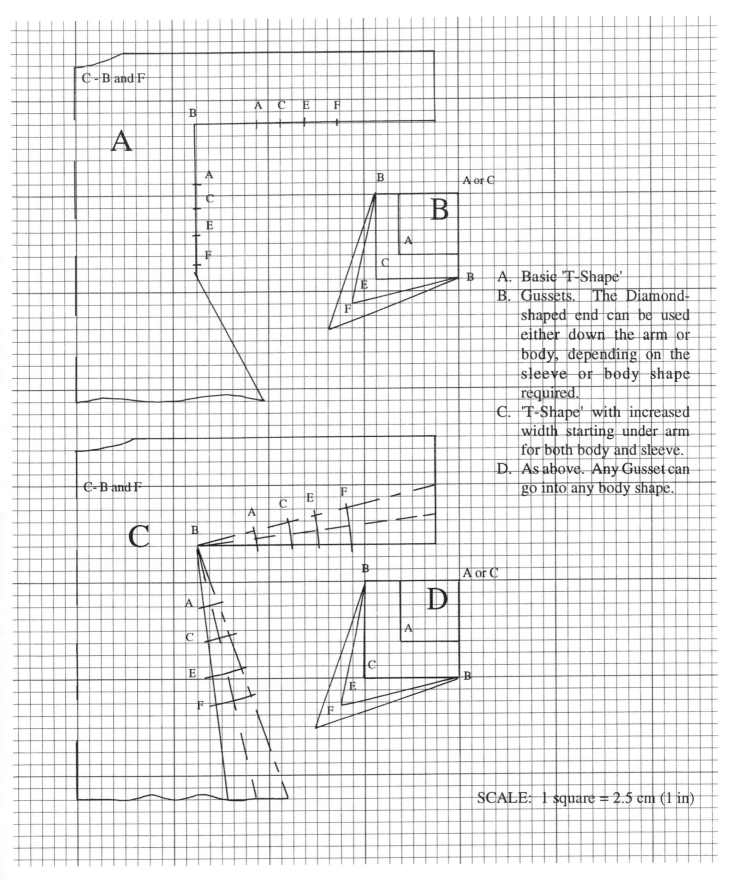

C - B and F

A

B

A or C

B

A. Basic 'T-Shape'
B. Gussets. The Diamond-shaped end can be used either down the arm or body, depending on the sleeve or body shape required.
C. 'T-Shape' with increased width starting under arm for both body and sleeve.
D. As above. Any Gusset can go into any body shape.

C - B and F

C

B

A or C

D

SCALE: 1 square = 2.5 cm (1 in)

PATTERN SHEET 8. This pattern has 3 body shapes and 3 different gussets shapes. The angle of the sides and sleeves of the body version 'B' plus the deep dolman gusset will produce the effect seen in costumes from the English Apocalypse. Compared the amount of fabric in this version with that for the pattern of the built in dolman armhole shown as a dash line on this Pattern. (See Figures 37, 38, 39; Plates 26 and 27.)

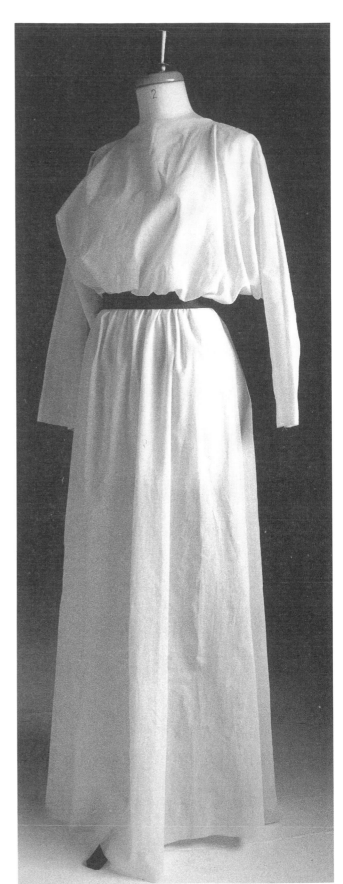

Plate 26. Toile for Pattern 8 using large gusset.

Plate 27.

Pattern Sheet 8. 'T-shapes' with Dolman Gussets

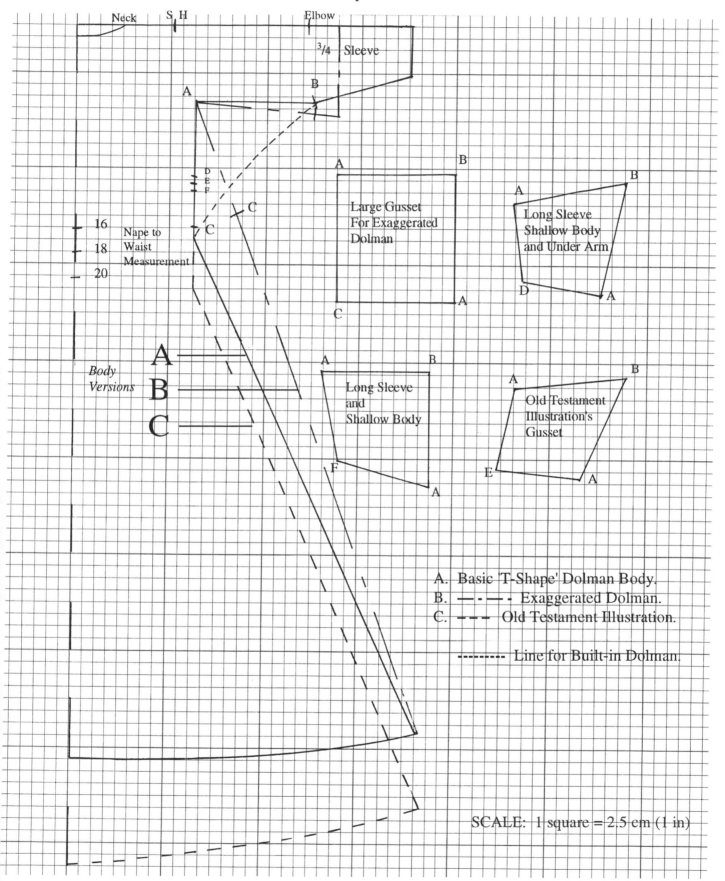

Neck   S H   Elbow

³/4   Sleeve

A   B

D
E
F

C

C

C

16

18

20

Nape to
Waist
Measurement

Body
Versions

A

B

C

A   B

**Large Gusset
For Exaggerated
Dolman**

C   A

A   B

**Long Sleeve
and
Shallow Body**

F

A

B

A

**Long Sleeve
Shallow Body
and Under Arm**

D   A

A   B

**Old Testament
Illustration's
Gusset**

E   A

A. Basic 'T-Shape' Dolman Body.
B. — · — · Exaggerated Dolman.
C. — — — Old Testament Illustration.

-------- Line for Built-in Dolman.

SCALE: 1 square = 2.5 cm (1 in)

PATTERN SHEET 9. This pattern shows an alternative cut for the shaped sides of the body of a T-shaped garment. If the side shaping is cut as a separate pattern piece, and put together flare to straight of grain, this makes the fabric push out at both the sides front and back, and flattens the sides, it also shapes the hem to hang more or less level at the sides.

Looking at the reproductions of patterns of very old garments this is not obvious due to the layout of the pattern on the page. But an early 17th Century shift in the Museum of London cut in this way, when made into a toile worked as explained above.

PATTERN SHEET 10. A lady from the Luttrell Psalter. This pattern shows the T-shaped pattern adapted to a specific design. (See Figure 42; Plate 28.)

For patterns for the kirtle or cut through fitted dress worn at this time, use any of the ideas suggested in the chapter on 'Draping a Toile'. The Sideless Surcoat is discussed in the chapter on 'Surcoats and Cloaks.'

Plate 28. Toile for Pattern 10. 'A lady from the Luttrell Psalter.' This plate also illustrates cutting a toile to the waist or the hip, which is then extended to the hem when making the toile into a pattern, as explained in Part I, 'Draping A Toile.'

Pattern Sheet 9. 'T-Shape' with Separate Side Godets

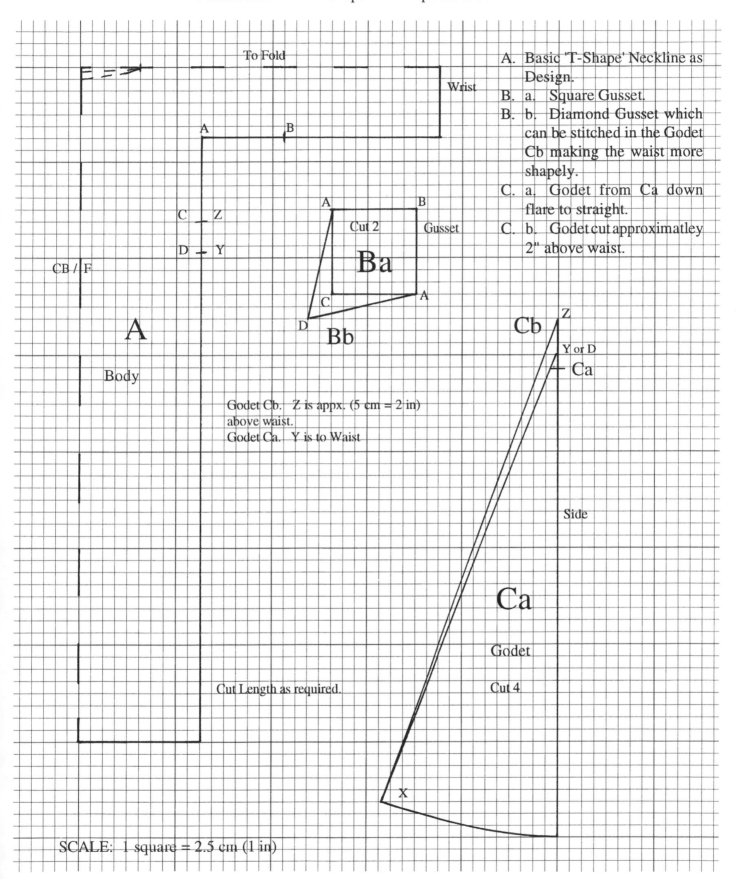

To Fold

Wrist

A   B

A   B

C   Z

Cut 2   Gusset

D   Y

Ba

CB / F

C   A

A

D   **Bb**

Body

Cb   Z

Y or D

Ca

Godet Cb.   Z is appx. (5 cm = 2 in) above waist.
Godet Ca.   Y is to Waist

Side

Ca

Godet

Cut Length as required.

Cut 4

X

A. Basic 'T-Shape' Neckline as Design.
B. a. Square Gusset.
B. b. Diamond Gusset which can be stitched in the Godet Cb making the waist more shapely.
C. a. Godet from Ca down flare to straight.
C. b. Godet cut approximatley 2" above waist.

SCALE: 1 square = 2.5 cm (1 in)

Pattern Sheet 10. Lady from the Luttrel Psalter

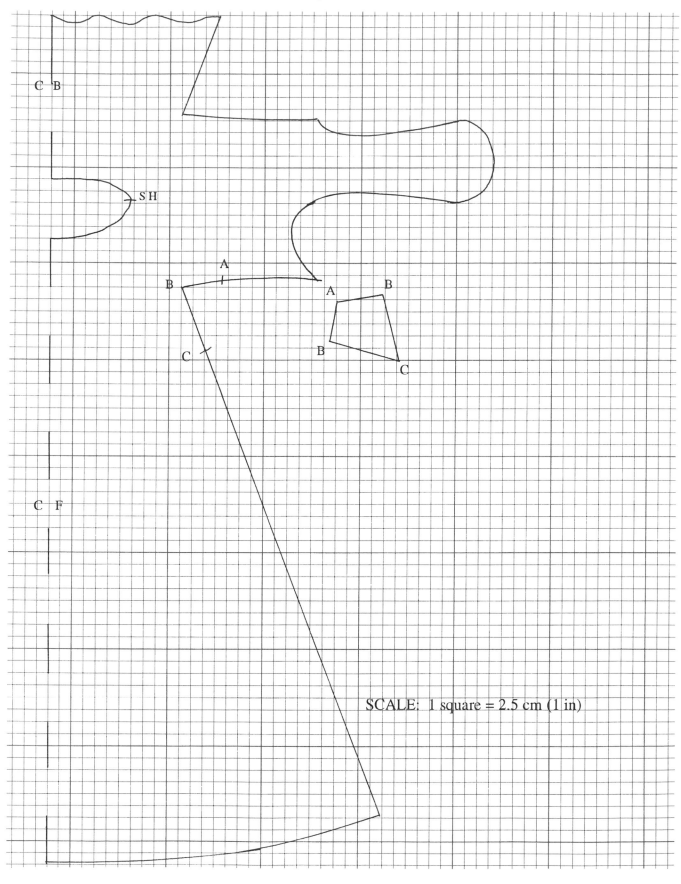

SCALE: 1 square = 2.5 cm (1 in)

9. 1400 A.D. - 1450 A.D.

Although the Hundred Years' War from 1337 until 1453 and the War of the Roses from May 1455 to 1485 ending with the death of Richard III must have emptied the purses of many of the nobles of the time, fashion as opposed to just clothes seems to have thrived. Clothes were now not only worn to keep people covered and warm, but were made in beautiful fabrics, elegant styles and sometimes were frivolous in design. It could be said that this period is the beginning of a designer age.

This is a stylish period to dress any play or opera, such as the history plays of Shakespeare, Shaw's *St. Joan* or Verdi's *Il Trovatore*. Each European style is now defined, the fashionable frivolous French, the wealthy Burgundians and the practical solid English are all depicted by Shakespeare in *Henry V*. By the end of the 15th Century, Spanish women were wearing the 'A' line farthingale which is well before the English and French. The Italian Renaissance I shall deal with later.

During this period some of the most beautiful *Books of Hours* were made, such as that commissioned by the Duke de Berry. The 'Trés Riches Heures', was drawn before 1415. Painters such as Rogier van der Weyden and Jan van Eyck in the Netherlands were now working in the more accessible art of the portrait style.

Men had been wearing the Houppelande, a large coat like garment, from about 1380, according to Cunnington's 'Hand Book of Medieval Costume', but by the beginning of the 15th century it was also being worn by women. This example from a brass of 1397, shows the high collar buttoned up the centre front of the neck (Figure 50.) The body of this example is left loose, but the

Figure 50. 1397. A Houppland drawn from a memorial brass.

77

Figure 51. c.1410–1420. (Above.) Figure from an English brass. Note Peter Pan Collar.

Figure 52. 1411–1416. A wealthy Lady from the Duke de Berry's 'Tres Riches Heures.'

houppelande was usually worn with a belt which is placed high, just under the bust. The kirtle sleeves which come to the knuckles protrude from the wide open ended sleeves.

The neckline of the houppelande is finished in three main styles, a high standing collar, a large flat Peter Pan type (Figure 51) or a long narrow shawl. There are variations within each style, created by differing widths of collar, and the width or depth of the neckline. A fourth style, mainly seen worn in paintings of the Virgin, is a round neck bound with a 2 cm ($^3/4$ in.) flat band, with 3 or 5 small cartridge pleats springing from the centre front.

This example from the Duke de Berry's 'Trés Riches Heures' shows the houppelande at its most stylish, as worn by a wealthy lady at play (Figure 52.) She wears a mid-blue dress with a red belt decorated with gold medallions. The hanging sleeves, lined with grey fur, are extremely long and have dags round the outer edges. The collar, which is only seen from the back is also in grey fur. She has a gold metal collar round the shoulders with two streamers down the back reputed to be made up of bells which tinkled as she moved. Although in this illustration she is standing up, the original has her riding side saddle.

The front view of Marie d'Harcourt (Figure 53) is also from a *Book of Hours*. The body of the dress is cut in one, from shoulder to hem, and the sleeve edges are dagged. Both the sleeves and

Figure 53. 1415. Marie d'Harcourt.
Duchess of Guelders.

dress are extremely long, and the neck line is finished with a demure white collar.

The painting by Jan van Eyck of 'The Arnolfini Marriage' *c*.1434 (Plate 29) is interesting to the costume maker, as it shows Giovanna, Arnolfini's wife, standing in repose showing off her beautiful dress, which is as clear as if in a photograph, making it easy to copy. I have made both the

Plate 29. c.1434. The Arnolfini Marriage painted by Jan van Eyck. The National Gallery, London.

costumes in this painting for a television play. The dress was made in a smooth wool velour cloth, but only the bottom twelve inches of the skirt was lined with fur. Even so, the artist found it unbearably hot under television lights.

It is a wonderful dress, simple in cut but the fine woollen cloth and its decoration make it very special. The front and back are each cut as one quarter of a circle, with the straight of the grain

down the centres. It is tempting to hope that the sleeve is also cut as a quarter of a circle but for many reasons it does not work. It is most successful when cut, as a raglan sleeve with a dart or gathering to get rid of the surplus fabric on the shoulder. The straight of grain is through the centre of the sleeve from the shoulder, with the front and back slightly off the grain. The width of the sleeve at the upper arm is about 45.5 cm (18 in) and about 76 cm (30 in) at the bottom. The split at the front of the sleeve is 2.5 cm (1 in) off the grain and the fur trimmed edge would stop the cloth from stretching. The extremely elaborate and heavy decoration holds the bottom end of the sleeve in shape. The pleats at the bottom of the split bring the hem back into line, if the pleats are not there, the hem line of the sleeve would slope down towards the front. The decoration on the bottom is a form of double box pleating (Plate 30) pinked along the outer edges, and then cut in from each corner of the square. The pinked edges show as a pale creamy colour, suggesting that the fabric was piece dyed rather than yarn dyed.

The pleats on the bodice form a sunray effect, being longer in the centre, graduating down as they go under the bust. They are no doubt stitched down or controlled by a tape to keep them in place, and covered by a russet and gold belt which is about 4.5 cm (1³/4 in) wide. The plain round neck is edged with fur, which means that this dress, if it has a fastening, would fasten down the centre back.

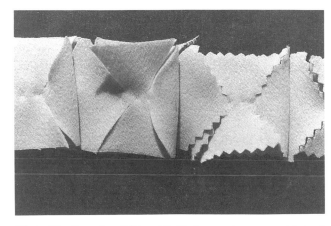

Plate 30. Sample of "Arnolfini" decoration; cut with both plain and pinking shears.

The skirt of the houppelande is lined or edged with fur, which appears to be longer than her waist to ground measurement. The train would probably have had a square end. She is not pregnant as art historians would have us believe. If you pin the corner of a blanket over a belt, and fasten it under your bust, then lift the 'skirt' portion as in the painting, you will observe that the thickness over the stomach is quite considerable. Take up the slight backward lean of the figure and consider what this would be like if lined with fur.

The under dress is made in a textured fabric in blue, but the fabric of the sleeves seems to have been ruched to create a richer texture than the skirt.

The end of the sleeve is finished with a narrow braid cuff, which matches the belt, and the sleeve is cut with a seam down the back. The bottom of the skirt is, like the Houppeland, edged or perhaps lined with fur. Observe that there is a tuck round the bottom of the skirt about 10 cm (4 in) from the hem.

Three bronzes taken from the collection of ten in the Rijksmuseum Amsterdam (Figure 54, 55, 56) show very good detail of the costume in the round, note the laced kirtle on the first unbelted figure. The museum dates these figures as 1476. In many books it is said they came from a fireplace, but the museum catalogue now says they are ten

Figure 54. From a bronze, Rijksmuseum, Amsterdam.

Figure 55. From a bronze, Rijksmuseum, Amsterdam.

Figure 56. From a bronze, Rijksmuseum, Amsterdam.

mourners from the tomb of Isabelle de Bourbon.

In the paintings of van der Weyden the houppelande can be seen in its many forms, with various necklines and with and without a belt. His 'The Magdalen Reading' (Figure 57) from the National Gallery in London, *c.*1440-50, shows the main features of this type of dress. The 'V' neck opening, edged with beige fur — which can be seen continuing into the skirt, both under the black belt and below her wrist — is laced over the same wonderful gold brocaded fabric of the underskirt. Inside the neck edge can be seen a fold of linen, which would keep the fur off the skin. The pleats of the bodice start above the bust, and are very

Figure 57. c. 1440—50. 'The Magdalen Reading' by Rogier van der Weyden.

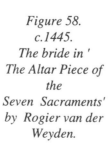

Figure 58. c.1445. The bride in ' The Altar Piece of the Seven Sacraments' by Rogier van der Weyden.

even which suggests that they are controlled in some way. The sleeves are set-in and are shaped on the seam which is placed at the back. This is indicated by the slight shaping from about 10 cm (4 in) up from the cuff (see Pattern 11.) This skirt is also lined with fur.

Another painting by Rogier van der Weyden, the bride in 'The Altar Piece of the Seven Sacraments' *c.*1445, (Figure 58) shows another variation of this dress. The neck this time is finished with a flat shawl collar, the belt is wider than the previous dress, but again the fur edge of the split can be seen below it. The pleats on this bodice start at about bust point level, again they are very even which suggests that they are controlled. The large hanging sleeves and the skirt are lined with fur, and the skirt of the underdress is lined or edged with fabric.

If, as in the drawing, the whole of the bodice of van der Weyden's painting of 'A Young Woman'

(Figure 59) were visible, it would be seen to have raglan sleeves and that the pleats of the bodice start from above the bust. These pleats must be caught into their pencil-like folds onto a lining, otherwise the fullness of the bust would push out and flatten the fabric (Plate 31, 32.)

Under some of the garments discussed above, the sleeve ends and sometimes the neckline of an

Figure 59. (Right.) c.1435. 'A young Woman' by van der Weyden.

Plate 31. (Above.) The outside of the bodice; showing the pleating for "A young Woman by van der Weyden.

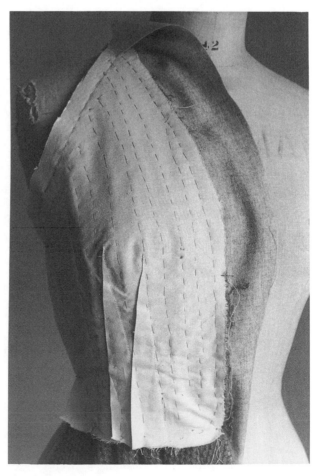

Plate 32. (Right.) The inside of the bodice showing the control for the pleating of "A Young Woman" by van der Weyden.

under garment can be seen. For a more complete view of what the undergarments looked like there are three paintings of Mary Magdalen by van der Weyden; each is wearing the kirtle and is painted from various angles so as to reveal a complete study of the garment. Because they were painted over a period of ten to twelve years, they are slightly different in style and detail, nevertheless it is the same type of garment with the same characteristics. Over the years he probably painted many models wearing similar garments, which explains why the chemises are worn in slightly different ways. In about 1440 he produced the side view, (Figure 60) although the shoulder and sleeve seams can be clearly seen, the detail of the front and back are difficult to see. The front view

Figure 61. c.1450-52. The front of the 'Mary Magdalen'.

(Figure 61), painted in 1450-52, clearly shows a long front bodice and waist length back — although the other two are short at the front and sides. The neck is finished with a band, which is mitred at the corners and is worn with a scarf or fichu inside the neck line. The shift can be seen at the head of the false sleeve and through the front lacing, which pulls the bodice tightly round the body. These examples are painted in a grey-blue and pale green respectively. In (Figure 62) 'The Altar Piece of the Seven Sacraments' of 1445, it is painted in red, from the back showing clearly that both the bodice and skirt have centre back seams. The 'U' shaped neckline is finished with a band like the front view, and shows a crumpled bit of shift, whereas the back neck of the side view is a square with rounded corners. In both the side and back views the skirts are cut separately from the bodices on a circular pattern. All the kirtles have a false sleeve pinned to the short sleeve as does St. Barbara in

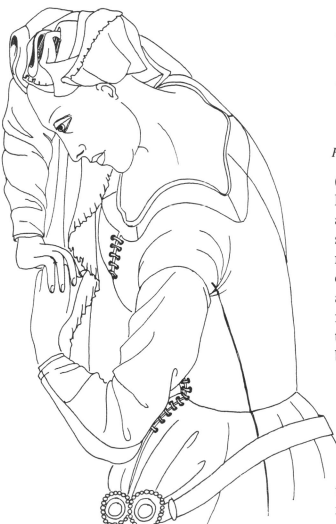

Figure 60. (Left.) 1435–1440. The side view of the 'Mary Magdalen', from 'The Descent from the cross.'

the 'Donne Triptych' in the next chapter.

The outrageous hat, on the figure wearing the front view of the kirtle (Figure 61), from a painting in the Louvre in Paris, is generally ignored by designers while costume historians refrain from comment. John Bloomfield in 'Churchill's People– A Wilderness of Roses' (Plate 72) decided to use this interesting style of hat. It appears to be made of a long coiled strip of fringed webbing, worn over a fine kerchief, the end of which is drawn down from the top of the head, under the chin and back up again as if to keep the hat in place.

Figure 62. c.1445. Back view of the Mary Magdalen from 'The Altar Piece of the Seven Sacraments'. Both bodice and skirt have center back seams.

PATTERNS FOR COSTUMES IN THIS CHAPTER

PATTERN SHEET 11. The houppelande can be made as explained in 'Making a Basic Dress' and the armhole can be altered to suit the style of the sleeve. The pleats can be stitched into place at the waist by pricking them on to a band on the inside of the garment. The fullness in the body and skirt will be dictated by the design, and the thickness of the fabric, and whether or not it is to be interlined, to appear as if it is lined with fur. There is no hard or fast rule and each costume will present a different problem (Plate 28.)

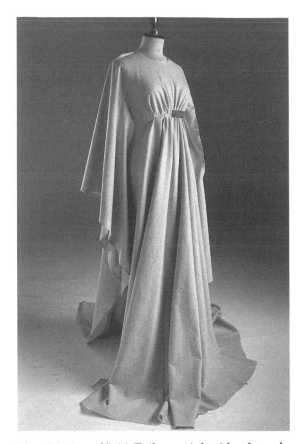

Plate 34 . 'Arnolfini ' Toile, on right side of stand.

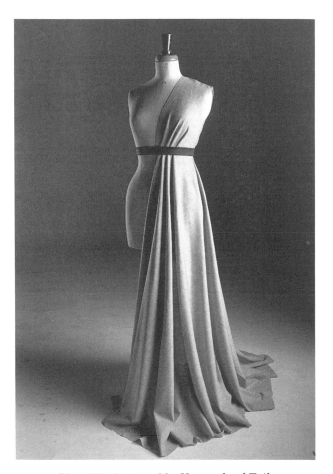

Plate 33. Pattern 10. Houppeland Toile.

PATTERN SHEET 12. The Arnolfini dress (Plate 29 and 30.) The underdress can be made from one of the patterns in the Toile chapter. If it is never going to be seen the simplest and least bulky shape that is suitable for the actress should be used.

Plate 35. 'Arnolfini ', Toile. Machined, left side of stand.

Pattern Sheet 11.   Basic 'V' Necked Houppelande

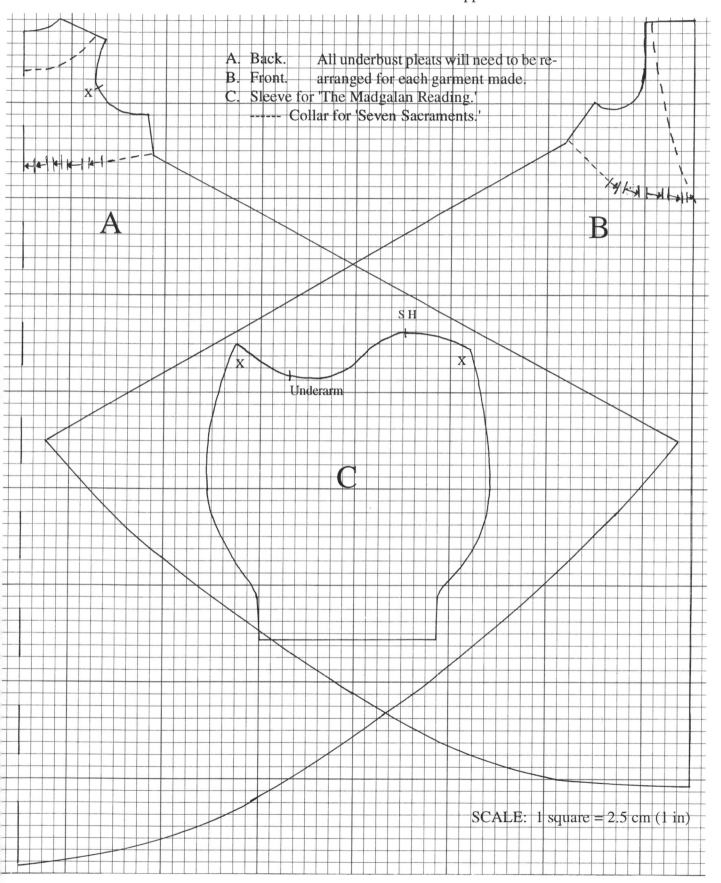

A. Back.   All underbust pleats will need to be re-
B. Front.   arranged for each garment made.
C. Sleeve for 'The Madgalan Reading.'
------ Collar for 'Seven Sacraments.'

A

B

S H

X

Underarm

X

C

SCALE: 1 square = 2.5 cm (1 in)

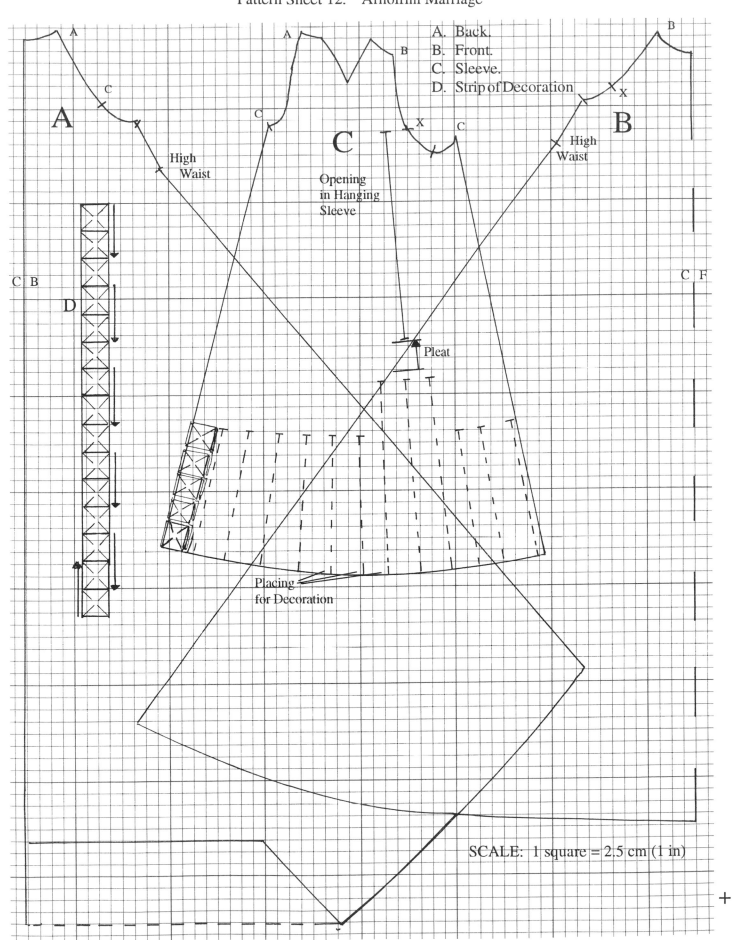

A. Back.
B. Front.
C. Sleeve.
D. Strip of Decoration

A

B

C

D

High
Waist

High
Waist

Opening
in Hanging
Sleeve

Pleat

C B

C F

Placing
for Decoration

SCALE: 1 square = 2.5 cm (1 in)

PATTERN SHEET 13. The Kirtle needs to be made in a firm but pliable fabric so that when it is laced together it will act like a corset. The bodice can be used straight round the waist or shaped down as the pattern from the side to the centre front. The bottom needs to be piped or turned ready to top stitch it on to the skirt (Plates 36, 37.)

If the bottom of the bodice is shaped, to find the correct placing for the bodice on the skirt after finishing the waist of the skirt put it on the stand, lay the bodice over it and draw the shape of the bodice on to the skirt.

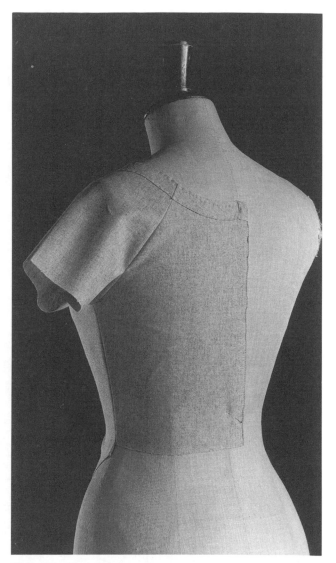

Plate 37. Kirtle Bodice. Back.

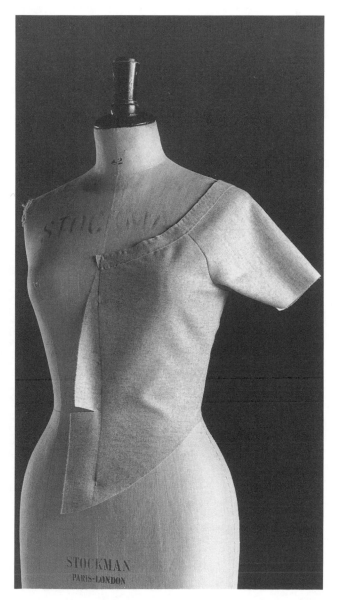

Plate 36. Kirtle Bodice. Front.

SLEEVES (Figure 63) 7 Sleeves.

The hanging sleeves which are a feature of early fifteenth century dress can be plain or full on the head, and plain or dagged round the edges. Because the fulling and raising of the cloth would stop it from fraying, and most of the edges that are dagged lie on the bias, the dagged edges could have been cut and not finished. Today this will only work if the fabric is closely woven and/or the edges are cut are on the bias, otherwise some other method has to be found to finish the edge. Very elaborately cut edges can be zig-zagged over as for Sleeve Number 1 (Figure 118), in the Italian Renaissance chapter.

Pattern Sheet 13. Kirtle. Bodice — Sleeve and Skirt

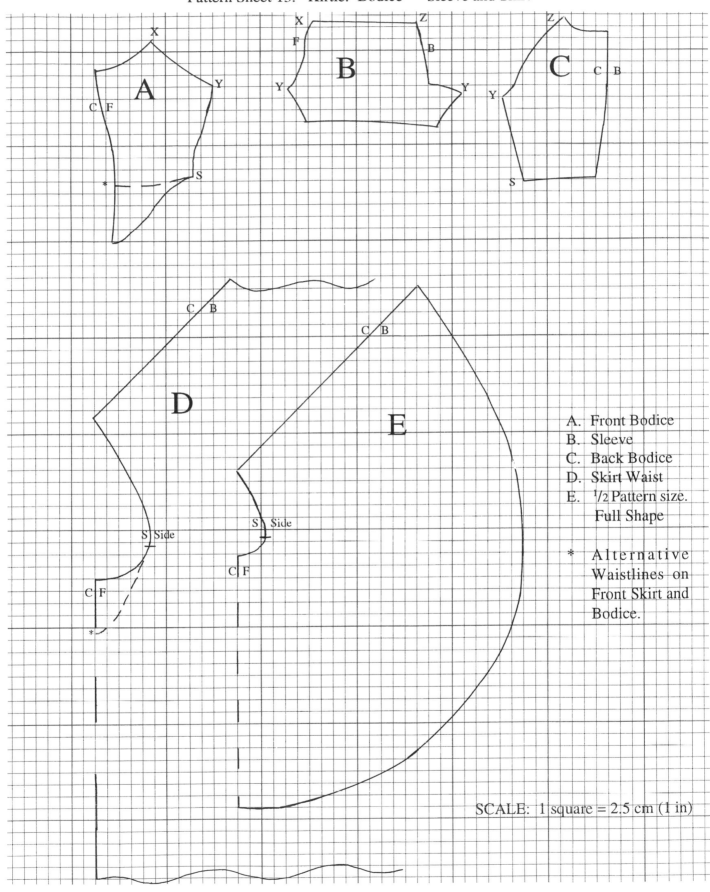

A. Front Bodice
B. Sleeve
C. Back Bodice
D. Skirt Waist
E. $\frac{1}{2}$ Pattern size.
   Full Shape

* Alternative Waistlines on Front Skirt and Bodice.

SCALE: 1 square = 2.5 cm (1 in)

PATTERN SHEET 14, 15, 16. **Sleeves** (Plates 38, 39.) With long hanging sleeves the secret is a good shape to the head of the sleeve, whether it is pleated or plain, so that the fabric will hang straight from the point of the shoulder to the ground. The length, width and shape at the bottom, can then be altered at will. The patterns I give are meant as a guide to the wide variation of both fitted and hanging sleeves of this period, but use these sleeves as a base, find some pictures, and experiment.

Hanging sleeves are the part of a costume about which a designer will get a fixed idea and use the same shape for everybody, but an imaginative cutter can suggest alternative styles and in doing so can contribute to the production.

Dagged sleeves are quite often lined with fur, choose the fur carefully. Find either a thin fake fur or, if a real fur is used, shorn rabbit will work.

To Make a Dagged Sleeve Lined With Fur

1.   If the sleeve is lined with fur, first shape the dags in the fur, it being the more difficult fabric of the two to deal with. Keeping the sleeve flat, turn in the edges all the way round and either bias in or turn in $^{1}/_{2}$ cm ($^{1}/_{4}$ in) and fell or herringbone back.

2.   Lay the cloth sleeve over the fur wrong sides facing, and tack them together. Make sure there is enough allowance on the fabric to manipulate it round the dags.

The next stage is very important.

3.   Pin the cloth to each dag, making sure they are all lying very flat, and clip the cloth as far as the top of the dags. If the fabric is apt to fray smear a small amount of a latex glue on to the wrong side at the top of each of the slashes, or if possible reinforce the corners.

4.   Turn in the cloth so that it fits neatly round all the dags and finish by felling it on to the stitch line or edge of the fur.

Plate 38. Hanging Sleeve. Pattern 15; Sleeve Da.

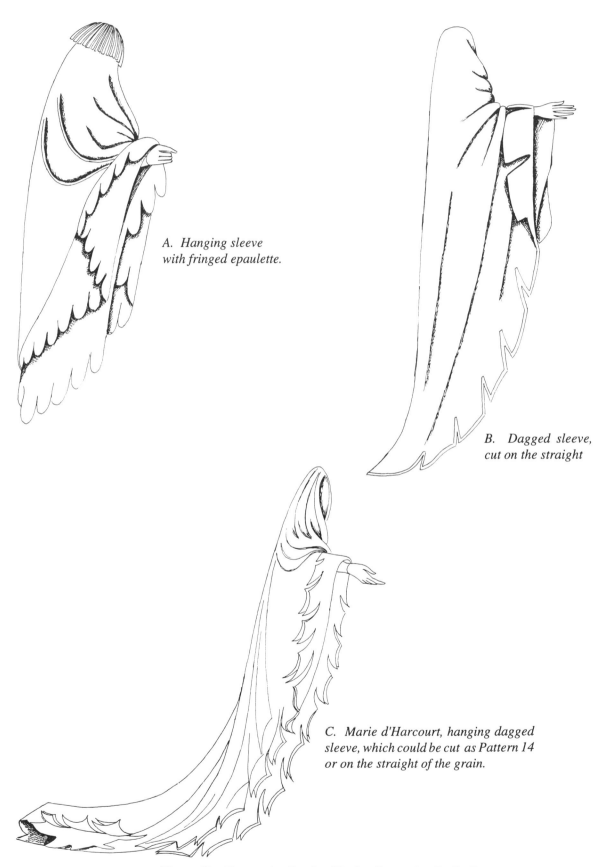

A. *Hanging sleeve with fringed epaulette.*

B. *Dagged sleeve, cut on the straight*

C. *Marie d'Harcourt, hanging dagged sleeve, which could be cut as Pattern 14 or on the straight of the grain.*

Figure 63. Sleeves A , B, C. (Facing Page) D, E, F, G.

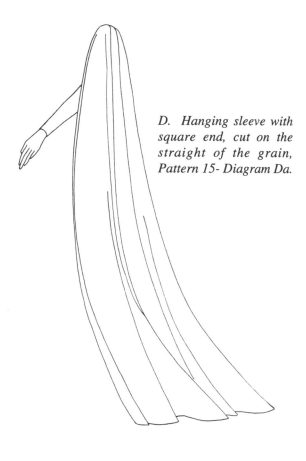

D. *Hanging sleeve with square end, cut on the straight of the grain, Pattern 15- Diagram Da.*

E. *Hanging sleeve with cartridge pleated head.*

F. *Sleeve with deep cuff.*

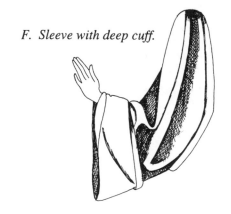

G. *Bishop sleeve.*

Once the dags are finished, take out the tacking at the head of the sleeve, ready to make up the front seam of the sleeve.

5.   To make up the sleeve and its lining, start at the head end of the outer sleeve. Machine as far as the join with the lining; go backwards and forwards at the join and then continue up the lining.

6.   Press the seam and tack the heads of the fabric and the lining together.

WATCH POINT
The way the lining is finished will depend on how far the fur goes into the head of the sleeve. It is adviseable to replace that part of the head of the sleeve that will not show with an ordinary sleeve lining fabric.

To join fur; trim the seam allowance off the fur, and oversew or zig-zag the seam together, machining the fabric lining together as usual. .

If the sleeve is lined with fabric, not fur, the main fabric and the lining can be bagged out, but all the acute corners will need reinforcing first.

Every new fabric and design poses a different problem and will therefore need careful thought.

Most sleeves for this period are smooth at the head or are cut as a raglan sleeve and can be put in as a modern sleeve. Those which are too full to be put in by easing or gathering can be cartridge pleated, using the method for Sleeve 1 in the Italian Renaissance chapter.

Sleeve G, taken from a painting, is very interesting, it could be a modern bishop sleeve fastened with a button and hole (Figure 63)—No Pattern.

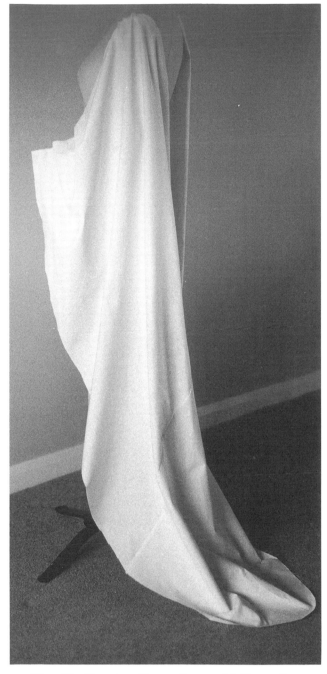

Plate 39. Hanging Sleeve, Pattern 16 Sleeve Ca.

Pattern Sheet 14.   B. Hanging Sleeve Cut on Straight of Grain
F. Sleeve with Deep Cuff

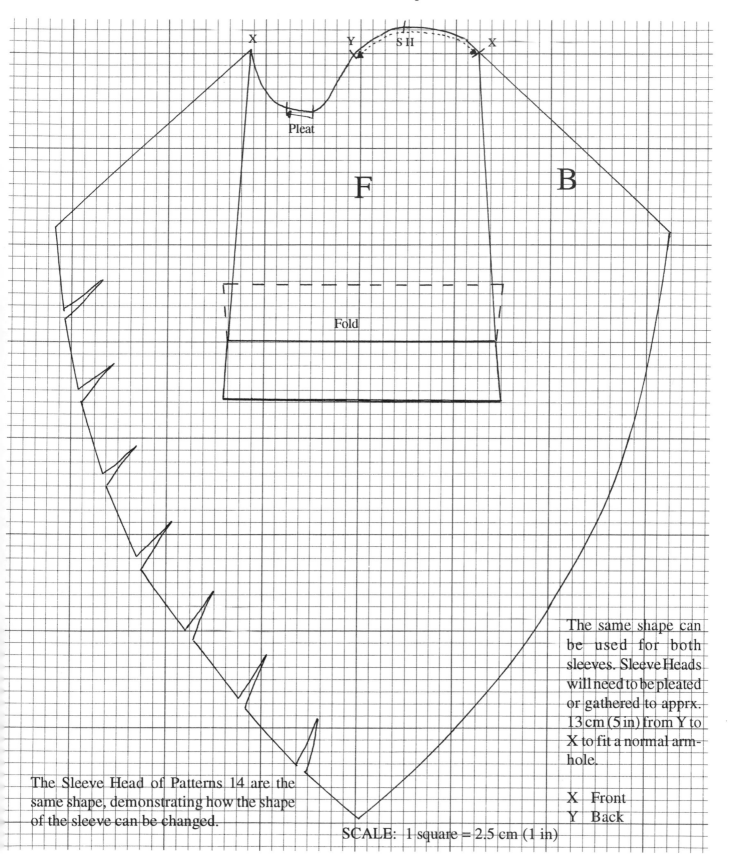

The same shape can be used for both sleeves. Sleeve Heads will need to be pleated or gathered to apprx. 13 cm (5 in) from Y to X to fit a normal arm-hole.

X   Front
Y   Back

The Sleeve Head of Patterns 14 are the same shape, demonstrating how the shape of the sleeve can be changed.

SCALE: 1 square = 2.5 cm (1 in)

Pattern Sheet 15.   Da   Hanging Sleeve Cut on Straight of Grain (Figure D)
Db   Hanging Sleeve Cut in Two Pieces

Da.   Sleeve open from Shoulder to Hem

Db.   Sleeve — as above — cut in two pieces with flare on the Back at 'Y' and 4 cm (1 1/2 in) extra at the Front 'X'

The Head of both Sleeves needs either pleating or gathered to approx. 13 cm (5 in) across the Head to fit into a normal armhole.

X   Front
Y   Back

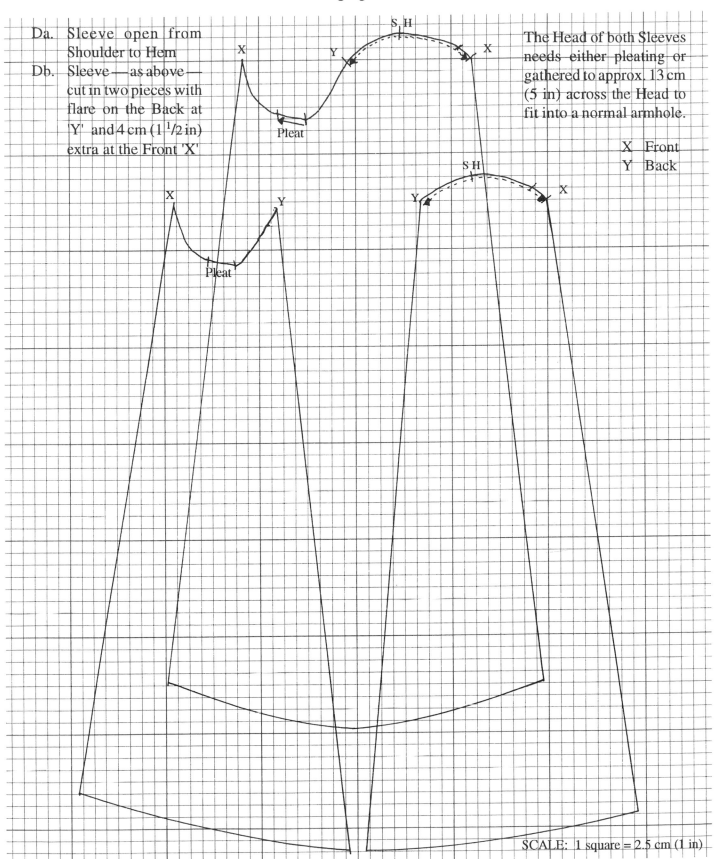

SCALE: 1 square = 2.5 cm (1 in)

Pattern Sheet 16.   C 1 Hanging Sleeve Cut on the Bias. C with Alternative End.

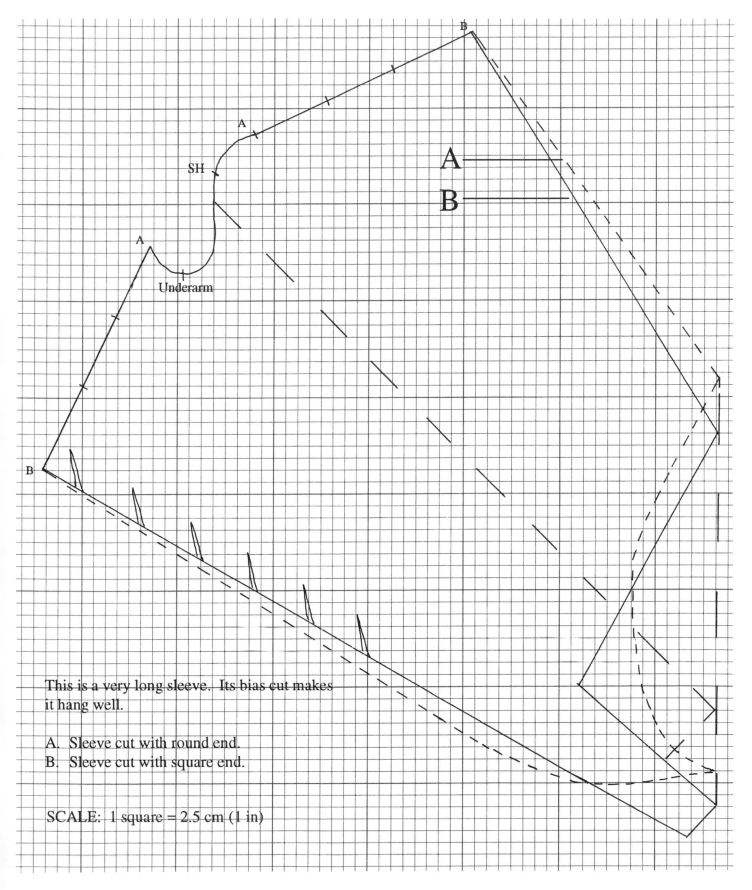

A

B

B

SH

A

Underarm

A ═══════
B ═══════

B

This is a very long sleeve. Its bias cut makes
it hang well.

A. Sleeve cut with round end.
B. Sleeve cut with square end.

SCALE: 1 square = 2.5 cm (1 in)

Plate 40 a.

Plate 40 a,b,c. Pelléas and Mélisande by Debussy, designed by Beni Montresor opened the 1962 Glyndebourne Opera Season. This was my first season as part time staff at Glyndebourne and I made for this production 12 nuns. In 1963 I went back as ladies cutter and the fragile dress worn by Mélisande, sung by Denise Duval from the Paris Opera, had to be re-made.

The design (Plate 40 a.) and the working drawings (40 c.) show a semi-fitted dress gliding over the body. It was made in two layers of silk organza, one of yellow under a beige top layer, over a white jap silk base. The original dress had been made with seams on a princess line, but the seams of the three layers, where difficult to keep on top of each other and showed very badly. This had to be remedied, so I decided to experiment and see if I could make a dress with no visible seams. My whole idea was a gamble and could have gone very wrong. I decided to cut all the layers on the bias and to steam the organza pulling it into a shape.

The jap silk was relatively easy as it was fine and pliable, but silk organza which is finished with a gumarabic dressing had to be treated in a different way. The dress was cut in 3 pieces with seams down the sides and the centre back, similar to that in Pattern 2 but with no centre front seam. I and my assistant, Merle Moxam, stayed each night after everyone had gone home, and steamed and pulled the organza into shape along the straight of the grain and then weighted it and left it until the morning when the dressing in the organza had set; little by little it took the shape of the stand.

The only visible seams in the end were those at the armholes. Using a set in sleeve, the three layers of the body and those of the sleeve were machined in together. The shoulder, sides and back seams were hardly visible from the auditorium. The dress was decorated with medallions cut from a cream and gold lame fabric, starting with the small motifs at under bust level and graduating to large ones at the hem. This turned out to be a very successful dress and Mme. Duval was very pleased. The working design (Plate 40 c.) shows the three variations of the dress worn during the opera. The character in the centre of the design is Pelléas (Plate 40 c.), this was made in velvet with lace motifs collaged on to it.

The second working drawing (Plate 40 b.) shows the young boy Yniold, sung by a soprano, and Geneviève the mother of Pelléas. Her dress was in dark red and black shot, Thai silk, which was overlaid with dyed cotton lace and in places backed with metallic gold and brighter colored silks, giving a stained glass window effect. These costumes were realized by David Harvey-Jones.

It was a memorable production both visually and musically and must have been one of the last productions to be mounted which was directed by Carl Ebert and conducted by Vittorio Gui.

Plate 40 b.

Plate 40 c.

10. 1450 A.D. — 1500 A.D.

For the visual examples of the second half of the fifteenth century, manuscripts and paintings of religious subjects are the main source of full length representations. In many paintings the ladies are often depicted kneeling with the arms invariably placed across the waist. Many secular portraits are quite dark making it difficult to see any detail, although they are a very good record of shoulder lines, exotic headdresses, and jewellery, much detail below the bustline is often obscured by the frame.

By the middle of the century we see the transition from the high waisted houppelande to the wide belted 'V' necked style of dress. The changes in style are gradual, and would no doubt, as with the all the periods covered by this book, overlap.

The bodice at the beginning of this period is cut through into the skirt like the houppelande, but it soon becomes cut as a separate item. The bodice is close fitting with no visible wrinkles, and the underbust is covered by a wide belt obscuring the method by which the bodice is shaped. I use flat pleats or darts, similar to those used in the early nineteenth century.

The collar comes in a variety of widths in both fabric and fur. Underneath the 'V' neck of the overdress, a stomacher or maybe the neck of the kirtle fills in the cleavage. The resulting square neck can be either low or high, wide or narrow depending on the position of the dress on the shoulders and the placing of the stomacher.

Figure 64. c.1448. The Queen Dowager. English.

The width of the sleeves varies from a loose sleeve wide enough to slide easily over the hand, to the long tight variety popular around the late 1460's. Nearly all styles reached the knuckles, and are either bound over the edge or finished with a band of fur. In the eighties the sleeves are again quite loose but now finish at the wrist with a backward facing fur cuff.

Most skirts seem to be cut as a three quarter circle and are longer than ground length all the

Figure 65. c.1449. The lady painted by Petrus Christus.

way round, lengthening into a train at the back, the end of which is shaped as a square or a point. Skirts can be faced on to the right side as well as being lined with fur or a contrasting fabric. The depth of the facing varies and I suppose the more money you had, the wider the band on the bottom of your skirt.

The under skirt which is seen when the dress is lifted, is usually finished with either a braid or a band of embroidered decoration. The occasional illustration of a dress with a skirt which is level with the ground can be seen towards the end of the 1480's, and is usually decorated with a deep facing of fur or fabric. I suppose this shorter version could have been a summer fashion, but the long dress with train is worn until the end of the century.

A painting from a manuscript *c.*1448 of the Queen Dowager (Figure 64) is transitional and shows a dress made in blue velvet. From the pleats both above and below the belt it can be seen that the bodice is cut through into the skirt. The bodice appears to overlap at the front and is held together by the belt, which has still not achieved its full width. The skirt of the dress is much more than ground length at the front and has a train at the back. It is held off the ground by being lifted up at the side front.

The wide open end of the sleeves are either lined or edged with fur, as is the skirt. If the skirt is lined with fur then it must stop before it gets to the waist, as the size of the waist appears too small to contain that amount of fur, unless the likeness was painted to flatter rather than to convey reality. The under dress, which just clears the feet, is red, and is finished with a band of gold embroidery which matches the belt. The sleeves which are also red, are finished with a fine gold binding. A red triangle can also be seen in the 'V' of the neckline.

This drawing of a woman from a painting by Petrus Christus *c.*1449 (Figure 65) also shows a cut through dress. It is made in an extremely rich Italian brocade of dark green velvet and cloth of gold in the typical pomegranate pattern. Russet coloured silk has been used for the collar, between which the body of the dress is laced together across the chemise. Under the belt which is about 7.5 cm (3 in.) deep, the bottom of the collar can be clearly seen curving away. The same silk is also used to bind over the end of the sleeves, no doubt to protect the brocade; the left sleeve has been turned back making a deep cuff. The sleeve itself is a cross between a raglan and a set in sleeve, the head of which is cartridge pleated into the bodice to lie just underneath the collar.

The next dress is from a painting of a donatrix again by Christus (Figure 66.) The dress is a deep red velvet with grey fur collar and cuffs, black belt and stomacher. Above the stomacher is a narrow band which is the neck of the chemise. This dress is slightly later in date than the last, which is indicated by the width of the sleeves. The neckline is now wider passing over the centre of the shoulder. Again the sleeve is set well on to the shoulder, but is not a true raglan sleeve. This type of sleeve set well on to the shoulder with a tight underarm, would give more freedom of movement than a raglan or a modern set in sleeve, but would probably not be as comfortable.

The two drawings from the 1460's, one from a painting by Simon Marmion, (Figure 67) the other from a manuscript by the

Figure 66. The Donatrirx by Petrus Christus. 1410–72/73. (Approximately late 1450's to early 1460's.)

Figure 67. (Right.) 1460's. The Devil by Simon Marmion.

Master of Rene of Anjou are at the extreme of the fashion. They are both cut with a separate bodice and skirt, the one with a very low stomacher showing the cleavage, is of the devil dressed as a girl. The other is Fortune, (Figure 68) who is not so daring as the devil as her stomacher is higher. Both have long tight sleeves; the devil has deep fur cuffs which come to just below the wrist but Fortune's sleeves are nearly to the first finger joints and are edged with white fur. Both skirts are smooth over the hip, the folds coming from what are probably full circular skirts, both are lined with fur. The devil holds her skirt tucked up under her left arm, and its beige fur lining can be seen for about two thirds the depth of the skirt. Under it she wears a gold brocade under skirt. Fortune's skirt is a typical skirt of the period banded with white fur.

The girl in the full length drawing is receiving a book, (Figure 69) and is dressed in black trimmed with white fur, the skirt is also lined with the same fur. Under the deep scoop of the fur collar, she has a red stomacher, above which can be seen the chemise. Under the skirt can be seen an ankle length black underskirt.

Figure 68. 1460's. Fortune from a manuscript by the Master of Rene of Anjou.

The costumes to be seen in the centre panel of the 'Donne Triptych, (Plate 41) of about the mid 1470s' painted by Hans Memlinc in the National Gallery of London, show the main elements of the period. In this painting The Virgin, is depicted, as is usual, wearing an old fashioned Houppelande. It has a 'V' neck and the kirtle and shift make the

Plate 41. Donne Triptych

Figure 69. 1468. Lady receiving a book.

square of the neckline. The hem is edged with white fur. She also wears a large red cloak.

Lady Donne wears a brown velvet gown, (which I would cut as a bodice and skirt). The sleeves which are extremely tight reach the knuckles and are edged with fur. The sleeve head is covered by a flat fur collar. The hem is also edged with fur which is minivered—meaning to Scatter or Powder the white fur with slivers of dark fur, usually used for cerimonial garments. The gown has a wide belt acting like a corset round the diaphragm.

Her daughter's gown, with no belt, could be cut straight through with no waist seam. The open 'V' fronts are laced together over the red kirtle, and in the square neckline can be seen a fine fichu or scarf.

Saint Barbara, who stands behind Lady Donne is wearing a green kirtle, the shoulder and sleeve seams can be clearly seen, as can the false red and gold brocade sleeve pinned to the short sleeve of the kirtle. She is also wearing a green cloak over her right shoulder. This type of kirtle painted by Van der Weyden is discussed at greater length in the previous chapter.

Over the three and a half decades this type of dress is in fashion, the width of the 'V' neck, as can be seen from the illustrations, can be cut close to the neck, and at all possible positions across the shoulder; at its most extreme, looking as if it is glued to the very edge.

The collar in most illustrations appears to be laid on to the neckline as there is not enough stand for it to be a 'grown on' collar.

In illustrations where the back can be seen, the 1490's collar is treated in two different ways. Either it goes down to a point, reaching to the top of the belt, and presumably covers the lacing. Or, it is in two pieces, one on each side of the 'V' neck of the bodice, showing the exposed centre back lacing. These strips of collar could be the forerunners of the residual white strips seen in early Tudor portraits such as that of Catharine of Aragon.

The back view, which is an amalgam of two sources, one from a manuscript, (Figure 70) shows the collar strips, the lacing and the train of the dress caught up to the waist at the back of the

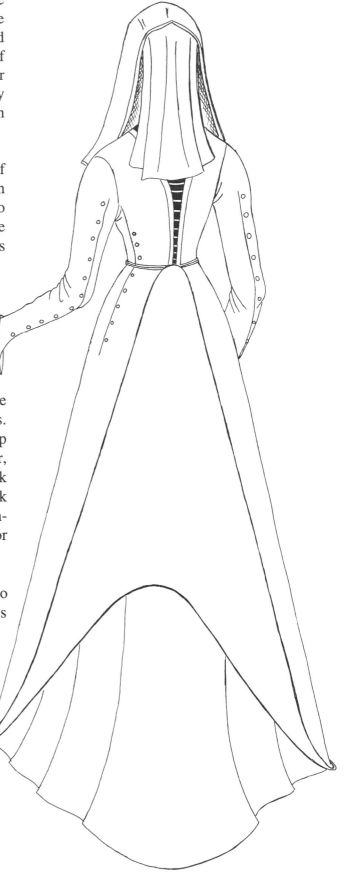

Figure 70. 1490's. This drawing is an amalgam of styles from two sources, the buttoned sleeves and bodice and the looped up skirt are from a French tapestry in the Musée des Thermes et de l'Hôtel do Cluny, Paris. The back bodice and again the turned back skirt, are from a French Manuscript 'Roman de la Rose', 1490, in the Bodleian Library, Oxford, England.

dress. The second from a tapestry, shows very interesting button fastenings down the sides of the body and the sleeves. Another drawing from a French manuscript shows a lady writing a letter. Although this drawing is early 16th century, it also shows the back of the skirt looped at the back over a gold belt (Figure 71.)

Figure 71. Lady writing a letter, from a French Manuscript of the early 16th Century.

By 1490 a firm bodice, probably artificially stiffened, is cut with a centre front seam. The neckline is finished by a continuous rounded collar, above which the point from the centre front of the bodice or an under garment often appears. The skirt, still cut using variations of a circle, was often straight round at the hem and finished with a wide band of fur or brocade. The sleeves finish at the wrist but now have a backward facing flared cuff (Figure 72.)

Well before the end of the century, the varia-

Figure 72. 1490's. Lady from a memorial brass showing the bodice or underbodice coming above the collar.

Figure 73. The series of Flemish Tapestries, 'The Triumphs of Petrach' in the Victoria and Albert Museum, London, from which these drawings are taken, show many variations of costume of this style. Not all bodices are long and some are cut through, others are much more like the earlier houppelande style with a belt either under the bust or at the natural waist. The front and back views illustrated here are taken from adjacent figures towards the centre of the tapestry the subject of which is 'The Triumph of Chastity Over Love.' The Tapestries are dated 1470 but were not finished until 1500-10.

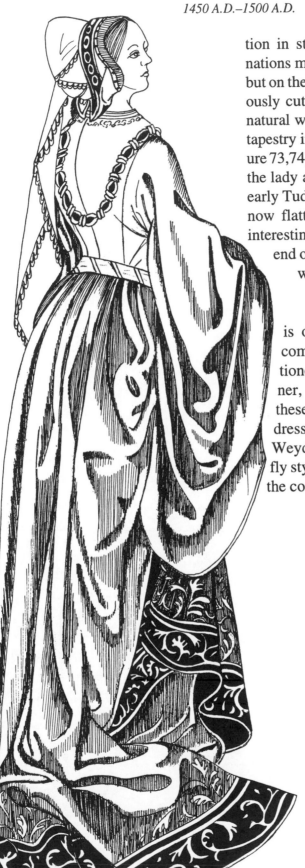

tion in style produced by individual European nations makes it almost impossible to generalize, but on the whole, although some dresses are obviously cut through, the bodice and skirt with its natural waist is with us. This example is from a tapestry in the Victoria and Albert Museum (Figure 73,74) from the second half of the century, and the lady at prayer shows the familiar style of the early Tudor period (Figure 75.) The firm bodice now flattens and pushes up the bust, and it is interesting to observe that it will not be until the end of the 18th century that a womans breasts will again take on a natural shape.

The piéce de resistance at this period is of course the variety of attractive and complicated headdresses. I have not mentioned headdresses at all, as I am not a milliner, but throughout the 15th century, it is these — starting with the elaborate linen headdresses painted by van Eyck and van der Weyden, to the later horned, hennin and butterfly styles — which are really the focal point of the costume.

Figure 74. Second half of the 15th Century. Back view of a figure from the series of Flemish Tapestries, 'The Triumphs of Petrach' in the Victoria and Albert Museum, London.

CUTTING AND MAKING

The cutting and making of the costume in this section falls into three main styles.

STYLE 1. Use the houppelande and sleeve patterns from the previous chapter for the costumes which are still cut straight through.

STYLE 2. The separate neat 'V' necked bodice, circular style skirt with long semi-tight or tight sleeves.

WATCH POINTS

This is a very simple style to make. The bodice is cut to the waist which is usually in a sightly raised position, and the bottom of the belt must come to the bottom of the bodice, the top of the skirt, is not then distorted by the belt.

If the collar is fabric, it must be made with a narrow inlay. After 'binding-in' the edge of the bodice, put on the collar as a modern loose collar. If it is fur, the fur can be finished on both edges and laid on to the edge of the finished bodice and the two edges whipped together.

Figure 75. (Right.) Early French 16th Century. Lady with large trumpet sleeves and a bodice, which is probably drawn together at the front by lacing under the centre front edges.

PATTERNS FOR COSTUMES IS THIS CHAPTER

Patern Sheet 17. Three bodice and collar patterns and a basic shape for a belt. The three bodice necklines vary in width from the edge of the shoulder to a shoulder width of approximately 7.5 cm (3 in) (Plate 42 a, b, c.)

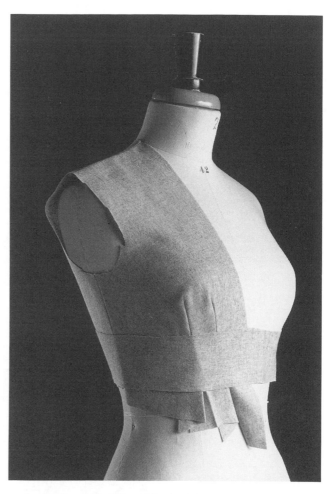

b. Bodice with full width shoulder; seams and darts machined, the belt in place.

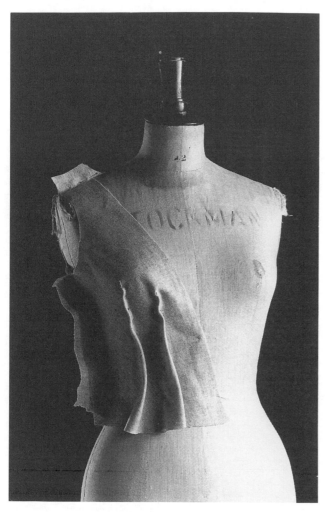

a. Mid-shoulder neckline toile, with side seam and darts pinned in.

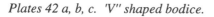

Plates 42 a, b, c. 'V" shaped bodice.

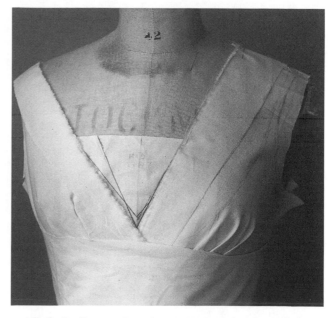

c. Toile Bodice machined with darts and wide neck on the left, and a narrower neckline with the bodice pleated to shape. A belt is in position over both.

Pattern Sheet No. 17.   'V' Necked Bodices

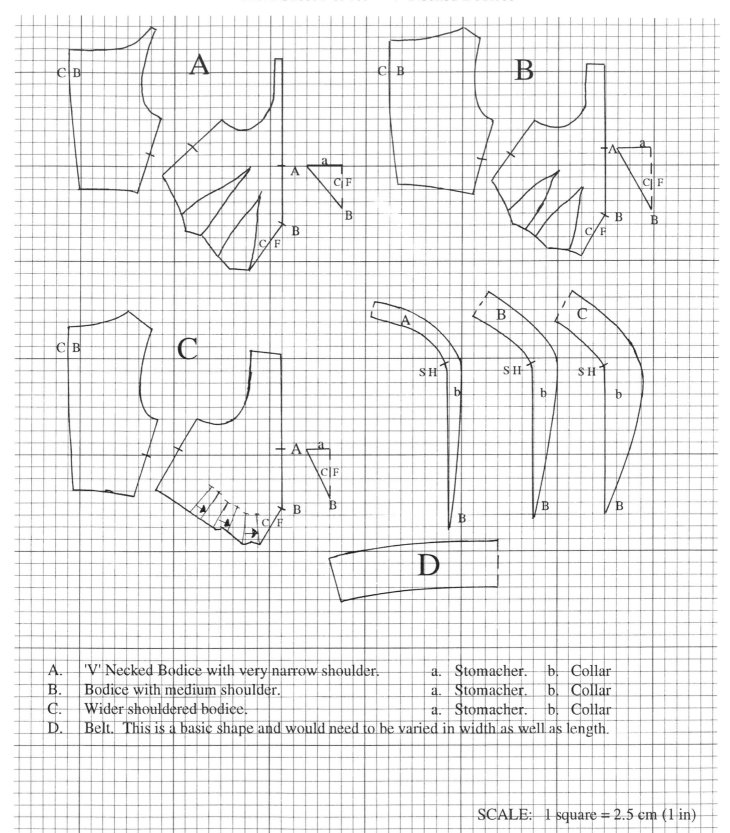

A.   'V' Necked Bodice with very narrow shoulder.   a.   Stomacher.   b.   Collar
B.   Bodice with medium shoulder.   a.   Stomacher.   b.   Collar
C.   Wider shouldered bodice.   a.   Stomacher.   b.   Collar
D.   Belt. This is a basic shape and would need to be varied in width as well as length.

SCALE: 1 square = 2.5 cm (1 in)

WATCH POINTS

For theatrical use, the stomacher front could be made as a separate bodice with a square neck, which would also hold the petticoat. Or, the stomacher could be stitched into the neckline on one side and hooked across. The front fastening will need a facing cut on the straight of the grain, and depending on the stiffness of the fabric, a bone may be needed to keep the fastening from wrinkling.

The bottom of the bodice can be 'biased in' or 'piped' and pricked on to the waistband of the skirt which is on Pattern 18.

Pattern Sheet 18. The Skirt.

STYLE 3.

Pattern Sheet 19. This type of bodice was fashionable during the last decade of the period and sees the beginning of the boned flat fronted bodice, usually with a separate skirt. This style is not so stiff as the later Tudor style. About 7 supple bones placed evenly across the front will be needed to get the desired effect, and still keep a curved shape (Plates 43, 44, 45, 46.)

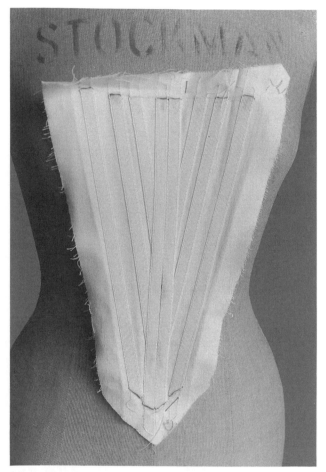

Plate 43. Stomacher made in drill, boned with 'Rigilene.' Shown pinned to stand. Used to cut Flat Fronted Bodices for all periods.

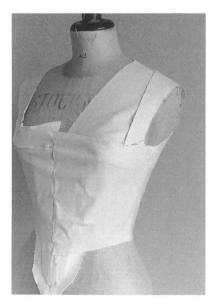

Plate 44. Bodice over partlet, cut over boned stomacher.

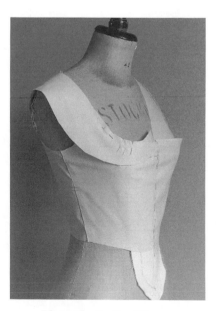

Plate 45. Bodice 'C' cut over boned stomacher.

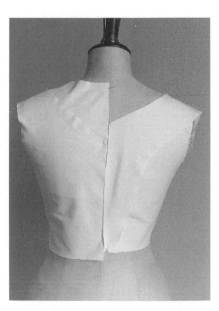

Plate 46. Showing Bodice, back, for Pattern 'A' and 'C.'

Pattern Sheet No. 18.   Skirt for 'V' Necked Bodice

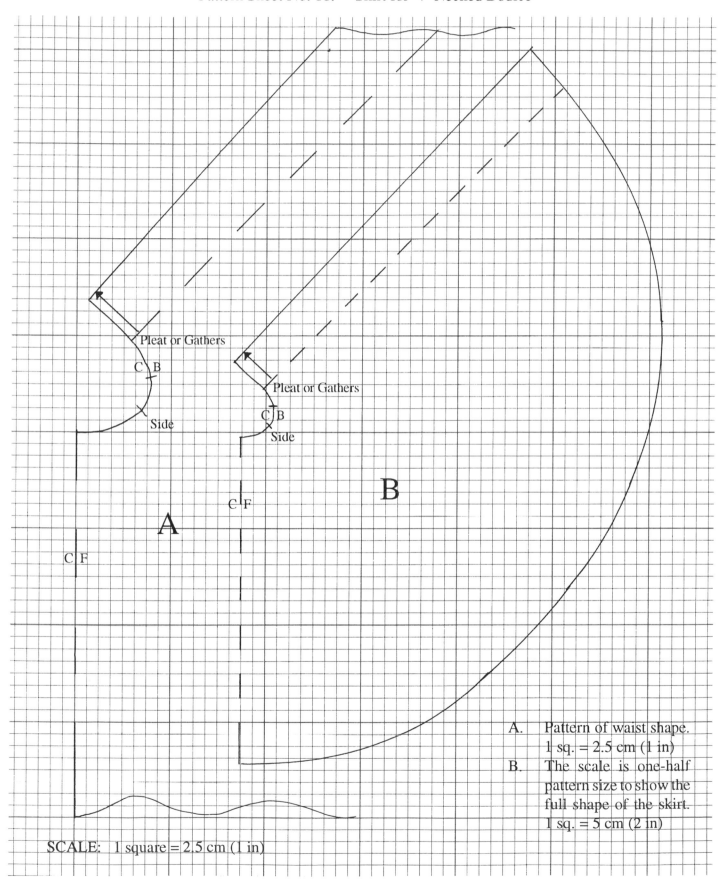

Pleat or Gathers

C   B

Side

Pleat or Gathers

C   B

Side

C   F

A

B

C   F

A.   Pattern of waist shape.
1 sq. = 2.5 cm (1 in)
B.   The scale is one-half
pattern size to show the
full shape of the skirt.
1 sq. = 5 cm (2 in)

SCALE: 1 square = 2.5 cm (1 in)

Pattern Sheet No. 19.   2 Flat Front Bodices, Skirts and a Partlet. *c.*1490-1500.

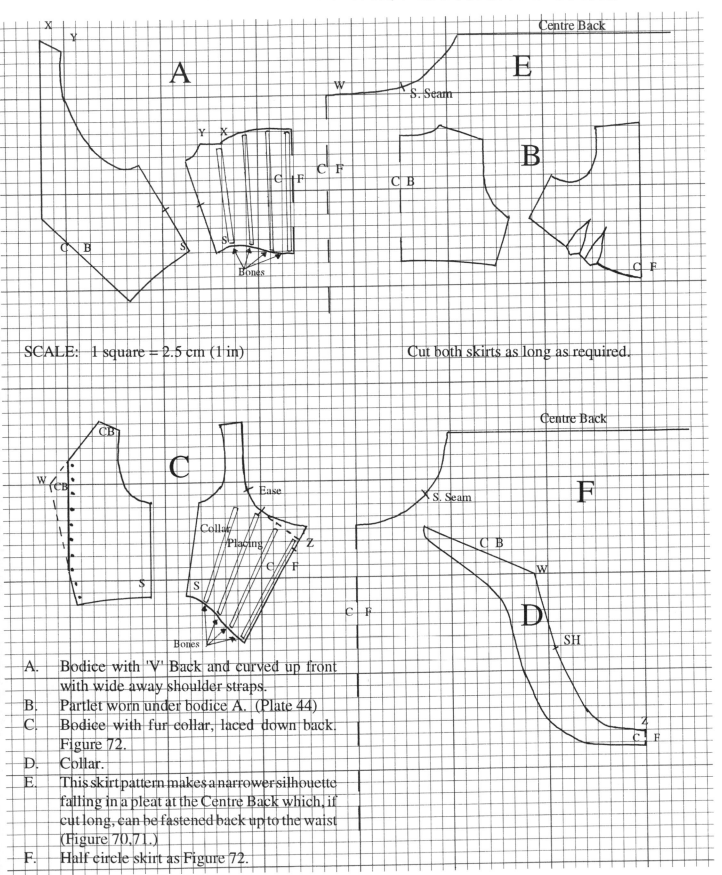

SCALE: 1 square = 2.5 cm (1 in)

Cut both skirts as long as required.

A.   Bodice with 'V' Back and curved up front with wide away shoulder straps.
B.   Partlet worn under bodice A. (Plate 44)
C.   Bodice with fur collar, laced down back. Figure 72.
D.   Collar.
E.   This skirt pattern makes a narrower silhouette falling in a pleat at the Centre Back which, if cut long, can be fastened back up to the waist (Figure 70, 71.)
F.   Half circle skirt as Figure 72.

Pattern Sheet 18. This pattern is taken from the Gothic Tapestries in the Victoria and Albert Museum in London, is difficult to date. The museum itself gives the date as the second half of the century, but to me, the costume appears to be of a style more towards the end of the century. The sleeve is built into the sidebody of the bodice, with the shoulder strap coming over from the back. The strap will need a stay tape or facing with a strip of fabric on the straight of the grain to stop it from stretching (Plates 47, 48.)

faced as surface decoration to the skirt, as well as being lined with contrasting fabric. If both hems are to be finished by hand it will take time, so unless time and money are no object, work out a method that will entail one round of hand sewing.

I have offered suggestions for finishing hems in 'Making a Basic Dress' but all fabrics and designs differ, so the finishing process needs to be re-worked for your particular design.

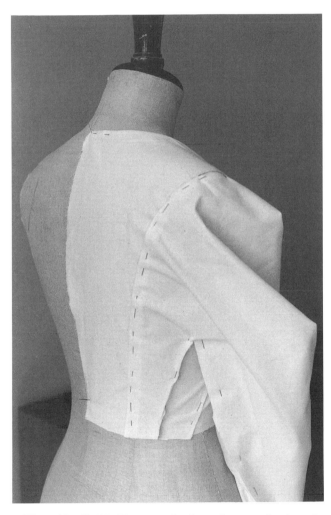

Plate 47. *Toile of the Gothic Tapestry Bodice, Front.*

Plate 48. *Gothic Tapestry Bodice, showing back and sleeve setting.*

WATCH POINTS

Most of the hems are circular in nature and all are extremely wide, many are also cut with a train which trails on the ground. Only the underskirts which are ground length need to be levelled to appear dead straight as most overskirts sit and trail on the ground. Some dress hems are both

Most sleeves for these styles are cut on the straight, but the long tight sleeves fashionable at the end of the 1460's will work better cut on the bias with a built in gusset. This sleeve can be made to fit very closely and yet still have enough room to move. See (Draping the toile and Making a Basic Dress) Part I.

116

Pattern Sheet No. 20.   Tapestry Bodice, Victoria & Albert Museum

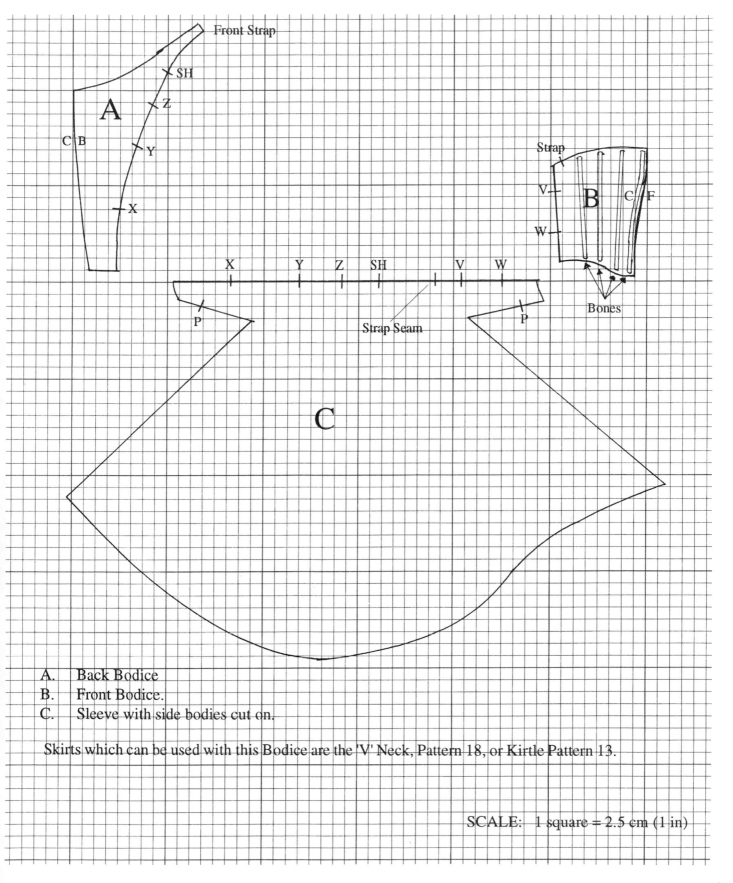

A.   Back Bodice
B.   Front Bodice.
C.   Sleeve with side bodies cut on.

Skirts which can be used with this Bodice are the 'V' Neck, Pattern 18, or Kirtle Pattern 13.

SCALE: 1 square = 2.5 cm (1 in)

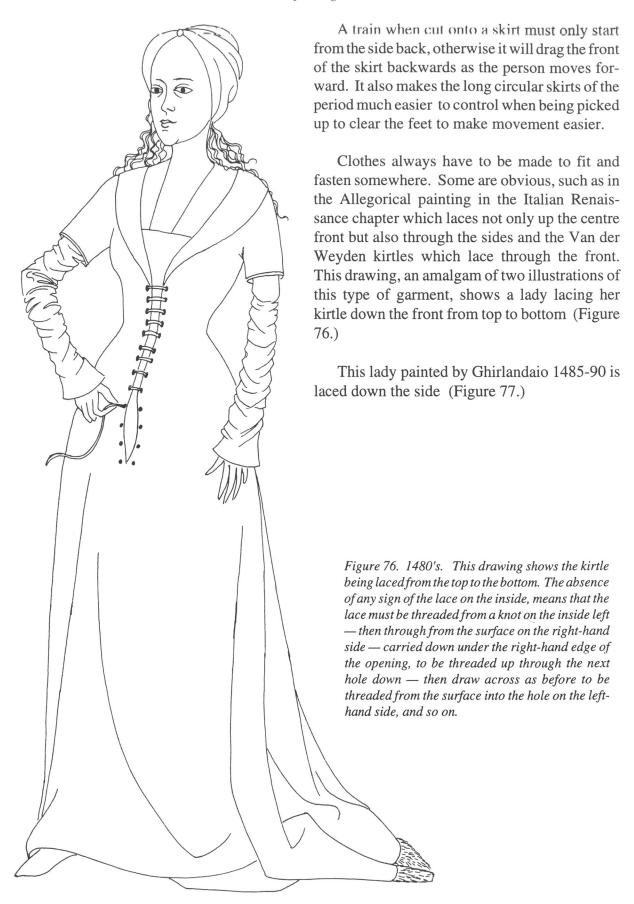

A train when cut onto a skirt must only start from the side back, otherwise it will drag the front of the skirt backwards as the person moves forward. It also makes the long circular skirts of the period much easier to control when being picked up to clear the feet to make movement easier.

Clothes always have to be made to fit and fasten somewhere. Some are obvious, such as in the Allegorical painting in the Italian Renaissance chapter which laces not only up the centre front but also through the sides and the Van der Weyden kirtles which lace through the front. This drawing, an amalgam of two illustrations of this type of garment, shows a lady lacing her kirtle down the front from top to bottom (Figure 76.)

This lady painted by Ghirlandaio 1485-90 is laced down the side (Figure 77.)

Figure 76. 1480's. This drawing shows the kirtle being laced from the top to the bottom. The absence of any sign of the lace on the inside, means that the lace must be threaded from a knot on the inside left — then through from the surface on the right-hand side — carried down under the right-hand edge of the opening, to be threaded up through the next hole down — then draw across as before to be threaded from the surface into the hole on the left-hand side, and so on.

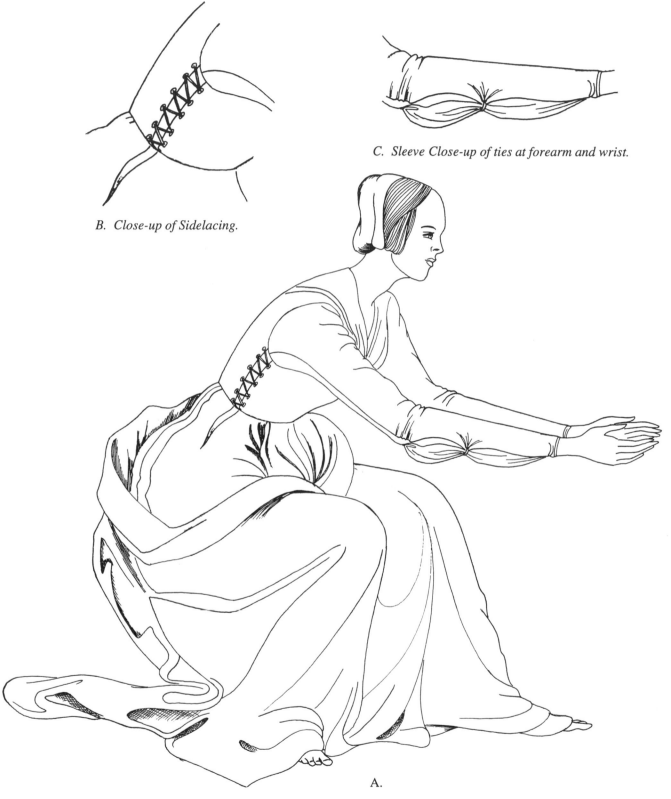

C. *Sleeve Close-up of ties at forearm and wrist.*

B. *Close-up of Sidelacing.*

A.

Figure 77. 1485-90. A. Lady showing sidelacing, re-drawn from a painting by Ghirlandaio. B. Shows the split side of the bodice laced together to get a tight fit. There is no mystery in this lacing as the method, using one lace, can be clearly seen. C. Shows the bodice sleeve being laced over the chemise sleeve.

Towards the end of our period, late fifteenth
century dresses wrapped across, as in the painting
of Dorothy (Figure 78) in her white dress, or laced
edge to edge under the centre front seam making
an invisible fastening as perhaps this the early
16th Century lady (Figure 75.) This type of
bodice would need to be stiffened to look so
smooth, and to keep the fastening at the centre
front so wrinkle free.

Closures unless meant to be seen must never
be intrusive. Look very closely at the paintings
and other source material of the period to discover
the 'way in'. It is usually the most obvious —
down the centre front. It must be remembered that
young women must have been pregnant for much
of the time, and would breast feed their children.
Look at the many paintings of the Virgin and
Child to see how this problem was solved, giving
a clue to were the fastening of the dress may be.

*Figure 78. 1505-1510 A.D. Dorothy, after the painting
of St. Peter and Dortothy by the Master of Saint
Bartholomew Altarpiece, in the National Gallery,
London. In the original painting, Dorothy is holding a
basket of flowers, which, here, has been eliminated, so
as to show the dress more clearly. She carries the skirt, of
the white dress, over her left arm, revealing the red and
gold brocade lining and an underskirt also in red and gold.
On the left side of the dress, the break in the neckline is
clear to see, and the front of the bodice wraps accross to
fasten down that side. The wrinkled, rather clumsy sleeves,
which are also lined with red and gold brocade, are tighter
on the upper arm than towards the wrist, but there is no
sign of an inner sleeve. In the neckline can be seen a
chemise or shift. The bodice has taken the shape of the
body and is therefore unlikely to be boned, the thickness of
the fabric and lining together would act as a corset.*

PATTERN SHEET 21. The last garment that must be mentioned in this section, is the chemise or shift as it is known in the next century. Unlike the later shift which is 'T'-shaped this one is cut with a raglan type of sleeve and gathered across the front, shoulders/sleevehead and back necks. It is often seen, as in this drawing from 'The Nativity' by van der Weyden of 1452-55, worn over another garment as a clerical suplice is today and not used exclusively as an under garment (Figure 79.)

Figure 79. 1452-55.
Chemise worn over,
redrawn from 'The Nativity'
by van der Weyden.

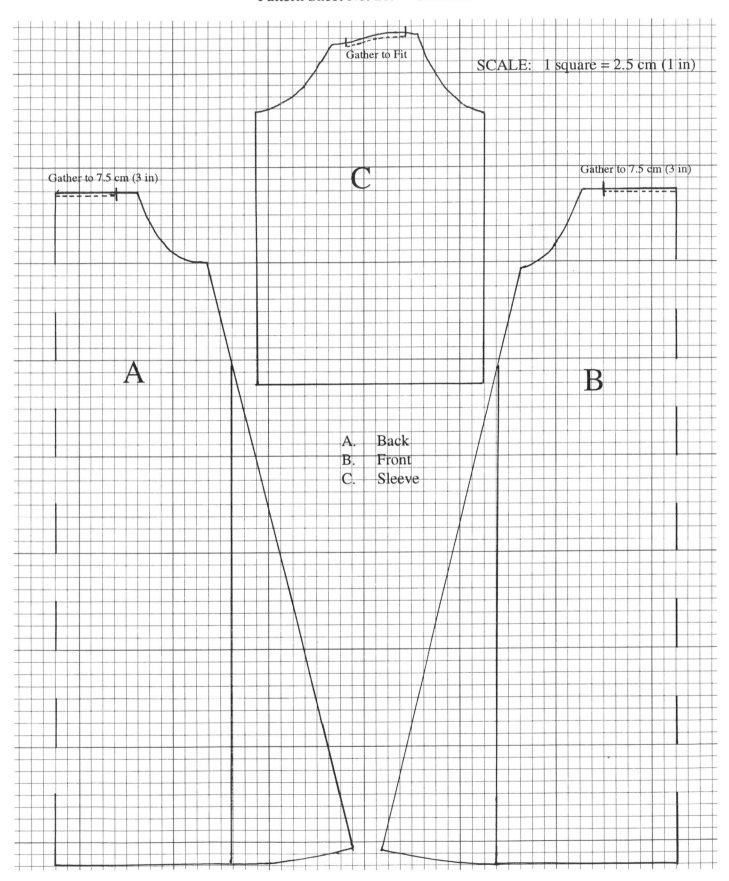

SCALE: 1 square = 2.5 cm (1 in)

Gather to Fit

Gather to 7.5 cm (3 in)

Gather to 7.5 cm (3 in)

A

B

C

A.   Back
B.   Front
C.   Sleeve

11. SURCOATS AND CLOAKS

SIDELESS SURCOATS

According to Joseph Strutt in his *'Dress and Habits of the People of England'* published in 1842 — 'the 13th century sideless surcoats could be long or short but were always sleeveless'; he shows an extremely short surcoat (not illustrated) as well as these two examples dated 13th century. The lady on the left shows the size of the armhole, with the hem of the skirt tucked into it (Figure 80.) The lady on the right shows an extremely long surcoat. The plackard of this surcoat — which

according to Cunnington's *'A Dictionary of English Costume 900-1900'* is the term for the front panel between the arm holes — is narrower than the first example. The skirt is picked up, I would think from about half way down, and falls over the arms in deep folds. The curious thing about both these figures is the kirtle hems, which look as if they have been pinned into pockets at intervals (Figure 81.)

In the 13th century manuscript *'The Book of Old Testament Illustrations'* the same form of

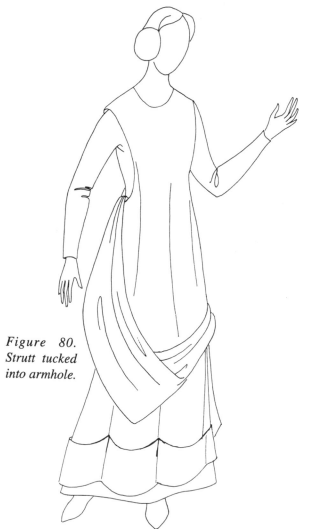

Figure 80. Strutt tucked into armhole.

Figure 81. Strutt with pocket hem.

'cyclas', the 13th century name for a sideless surcoat, can be seen (Figure 82.) In this example the woman is carrying grain or small fruits in her skirt by holding it up at the front, which also allows us to see her horizontally striped stockings. It has a plain round neck and the armholes are still quite small slits. All these examples would probably need some kind of opening to get the head through, perhaps on the shoulder.

Figure 82. (Left.) Cyclas from 'The Book of Old Testament'

Figure 83. (Right.) Margaret de Walksokne.

This type of garment seems to make recurring appearances from at least the 10th century onwards. It was probably like the cardigan is today, always there but only seen in quantity when it was in fashion.

By 1349 the armholes of the surcoat had become larger, as can be seen in the brass of Margaret de Walksokne in St Margaret's, Lynn Regis, Norfolk (Figure 83) which shows a very beautiful costume. The fabric of the dress is patterned with a tracery of leaves, and tiny buttons fasten the very

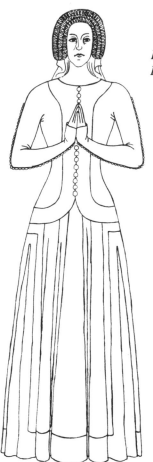

*Figure 84. 1375.
Lady Margaret Cobham.*

be on shoulders, but the skirt could be seamed either, down the sides, or at the sides front and back. It looks as if there is fullness eased at the hip, but it is more likely to be a flat pleat, which is the usual way to keep this style of surcoat tight round the hip.

By 1375 the standing figure from a brass of Lady Margaret of Cobham (Figure 84) has a narrow plackard bodice which is shaped up at the bottom and a row of buttons down the centre. The opening could be practical but there is no sign of button holes. The skirt is made up of a half circle at both the front and the back, the seams being left open for nine tenths of their length. The hem and splits in the skirt are bagged out with a facing which is turned on to the surface.

The kneeling figure of Queene Jeanne de Bourbon c.1373-8 (Figure 85) wears a similar surcoat seen from the side which shows the armhole open-

tight sleeves as far as the elbow. The edges of the armholes and the hem of the surcoat are finished with an embroidered band, and it is lined with yet a different patterned fabric. Her half circle cloak is lined with fur and its edge is also finished with the embroidered band. This is a most beautiful and rich ensemble.

The plackard in this example is narrower than those of the 13th century, but slightly wider than that of Lady Cobham of 1375. The skirt is still long and she holds it up off the ground by tucking it under her right arm, which seems to be the usual way of keeping long costumes clear of the feet. From the quality of the drapery the fabric seems softer than later versions. The whole garment slides easily over the figure and does not give the fitted appearance of Lady Cobham. The wimple covers the neck and shoulder lines but they must be similar to that of Lady Luttrell c.1335-40, (Figure 41.)

The seams in the Walksokne surcoat will

*Figure 85. 1373-78.
Queene Jeanne de Bourbon.*

ings to be quite wide. The front and back plackard fit closely to the body. The pleat at the side which keeps it snug on the hip line can be clearly seen. The kirtle underneath has either a belt or shaped seam round the hip, as does the drawing of the 14th century kirtle from Strutt, showing the purse hung from the belt (Figure 86.) Both kirtles have long, tight sleeves finishing at the wrist.

Figure 86.
Kirtle from Strutt.

they would not have been easy to do up through the thick fur, but they could be a type of stud, both methods would be difficult to use but not impossible.

The fifth example *c.*1448-53 is of Salome from van der Weyden's 'The Beheading of St John the Baptist' (Figure 88, 89.) As befits her character she is more exotically dressed than the others, and wears more the type of costume that a modern designer would go for. The surcoat is narrower across the shoulders than the earlier versions, the right sleeve seam, of the underdress, being just visible. The armholes which are more pointed at the bottom are banded with fur which make the plackard look narrower than it actually is; the bands also do not meet at the bottom. The neckline is a 'V' which is unusual, and is edged in white; the

Figure 87.
Ceremonial
surcoat of Jeanne
de Bourbon.

The fourth figure, again of Jeanne de Bourbon c.1388, (Figure 87) shows the surcoat as a ceremonial garment. The plackard bodice is made in fur and applied on top of the hip pieces, there are large ornamental brooches or buttons down the front and the skirt is very long and full. The under dress has a jewelled belt and the sleeves are now coming over the hand as far as the knuckles. The two garments fit so closely together that I think the buttons or brooches must have served some purpose apart from decoration, although as buttons back neck is square and drawn from a small representation of her in the depth of the painting. This garment shows clearly the square ended train that many dresses of this period have. The surcoat front shows quite a lot of fullness coming from the centre, suggesting that it is cut from a quarter of a circle, the side is split from about 23 cm (9 in) down from the armhole to the hem. The square corners of both the front and back hems can be clearly seen.

The gown underneath has short sleeves which are finished with a jewelled band, as also are the square neck and the hem. She also has hanging sleeves in a finer fabric than the rest of the costume, which come from beneath the short sleeves. She wears the gown either over a kirtle which has

Figure 88. Front view , 'Salome" , by van der Weyden.

Figure 89. Rear view of 'Salome'.

skin tight pink sleeves which finish at the wrist or false sleeves attached to the short sleeves of the gown. The skirt of the surcoat is tucked up on to her left hip showing the fur lining.

Another surcoat with a design difference is one drawn from Millia Davenport, 'A Book of Costume', number 834, page 316 (Figure 90), which is taken from a Franco-Flemish manuscript *c.*1448. The armholes are quite narrow and square at the bottom, the skirt is extremely long and either

Figure 91. Surcoat from the Brussels Master of the Joseph, Sequence.

Figure 90 Surcoat from a Franco-Flemish manuscript.

edged or lined with fur. It has a wide square neck which is quite low. A pleat, or fold of fabric, could be fullness as (Figure 91) can be glimpsed down the centre front. It is worn over a short sleeved gown, which as above, has either a kirtle underneath or long tight false sleeves which come over the hand to the knuckles.

The last surcoat is from an altarpiece by The Brussels Master of the Joseph Sequence in The Cloisters, Metropolitan Museum, New York. Dated by Max J. Friedländer, *c.*1470-1500 (Figure 91) although the costume looks earlier than this date. The surcoat or the kirtle, seems to have hanging sleeves, the left one she holds against her body together with the surcoat skirt to keep them off the ground. The centre front of this surcoat, I suspect, is what the 1448 version (Figure 90) above looks like. The kirtle sleeves finish at the wrist, and the skirt is level with the ground. She also wears a half circle cloak.

The three small drawings copied from Joseph Strutt (Figures 92, 93, 94), all from the 14th century, show (a) the back of a surcoat which quite obviously does not fit close to the body at the back, (b) a shorter simpler version of the 'Salome' type of armhole, also with a split up the side, (c) a ceremonial surcoat which has a narrow plackard which hangs close to the body at the front, and a very wide back which stands away and would look and behave like a train.

FABRICS

The narrowness of the plackard body against the weight and size of the skirt pattern pieces make the surcoat a difficult garment to control. They can be made from a wide range of types and weights of fabric, but the weave must be firm. If it is to be a garment to keep a character warm, then a heavily hanging wool or a fabric which will simulate one will be needed. A surcoat such as Lady Luttrell's (Figure 41) with armorial bearings on it, should be made in a smooth cloth which is suitable for dying and printing. The 'Salome' could be made in panné or velvet if cut on the straight, or, if cut on the bias, an evenly woven firm

Three drawings from Strutt.

Figure 92. The lady is carrying the train of her dress which is cut so that there is fullness from a high waist, suggesting that it is cut from a quarter circle.

Figure 93. This drawing shows a different type of surcoat altogether, being short and fitted, the side being caught together at the hip to make a large armhole and side split skirt.

Figure 94. A drawing of a ceremonial surcoat, showing a plackard which could be buttoned to the dress underneath. This would keep the surcoat, with its wide shoulders and loose back, in place.

fabric. If the weave is too loose it will droop and drop, so unless this is the effect the designer wants, the weave and fibre of the fabric, must be firm. If the fabric has to be mounted take care to let the skirt section drop without putting weight on the plackard which will stretch out of shape.

The lining must complement the main fabric in weight, a firmly woven poult or evenly woven man made slippy fabric that is not too thin will work best. Remember that the fabric of the kirtle and the lining of the surcoat must complement each other, try not to have either two slippy or two sticky fabrics next to each other.

PATTERNS FOR COSTUMES IN THIS CHAPTER

TO DRAPE THE TOILE

The fabric for most surcoats is cut on the straight of the grain — which I shall call Method 1 — but for those such as the 'Salome' surcoat painted by van der Weyden, these could be cut on the bias, I shall call this Method 2.

PATTERN SHEET 22. Method 1. Cut on the Straight.

Lady Luttrell surcoat (Figure 41, page 63 and Plate 49) and 'Cyclas' (Figure 82, page 124.)

1. Pin the fabric on the straight of the grain to the centre line of the stand, do this at both the front and back.

2. Pin the front and back shoulders together and the side seam from a low waist for about 25 cm (10 in) below the hip.

3. Having looked at the design and discussed with the designer the width and shape of the plackard, armholes and the neckline, draw the shapes on to the fabric. Do this at both the front and the back.

4. Cut out the surplus fabric from the neck and armholes, leaving about 5 cm (2 in) to play with. This will release the tension allowing you to see whether the plackard is lying flat, and make any alterations required.

5. Decide where the skirt seams are to be — side, or sides front and back — and shape the skirt panels to the width required, adding wheel pieces where necessary, or if the fabric allows, cut the whole of the skirt on to the bottom of the plackard bodice.

6. To finish the toile, clip into the neck and armhole curves. Turn in the allowance to the pencil line and pin in, so that you can see the shape clearly and adjust the shoulder seam again if necessary. With the stand at the correct nape to ground measurement, trim the hem to the correct length.

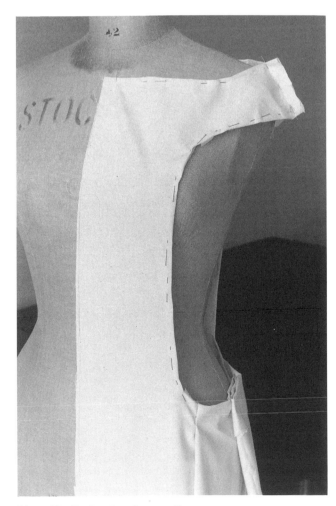

Plate 49. Toile of Lady Lutrell surcoat.

Pattern Sheet No. 22.   Lady Lutrell Surcoat and Cyclas

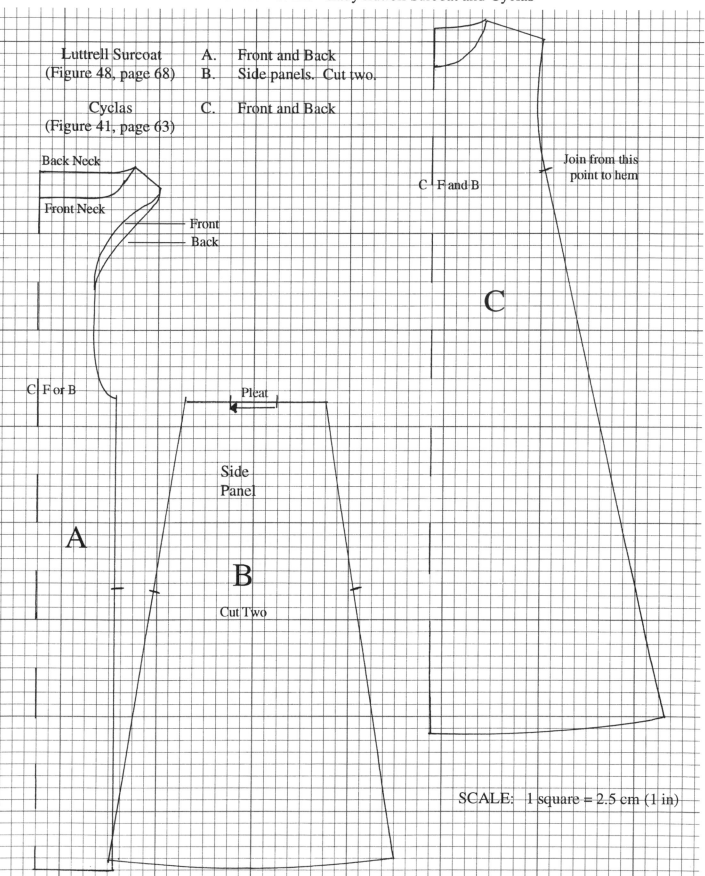

Luttrell Surcoat   A.   Front and Back
(Figure 48, page 68)   B.   Side panels. Cut two.

Cyclas   C.   Front and Back
(Figure 41, page 63)

Back Neck

Front Neck

Front
Back

C F and B

Join from this
point to hem

C

C F or B

Pleat

Side
Panel

A

B

Cut Two

SCALE: 1 square = 2.5 cm (1 in)

Pattern Sheet 23. Lady Cobham (Plate 50.) The front skirt could also be cut with the centre front on the bias bringing the sides onto the straight of the grain. (A quarter circle.) This would make the front slightly less full than the pattern. This surcoat can be made in a similar way to that in Pattern 23, page 133.

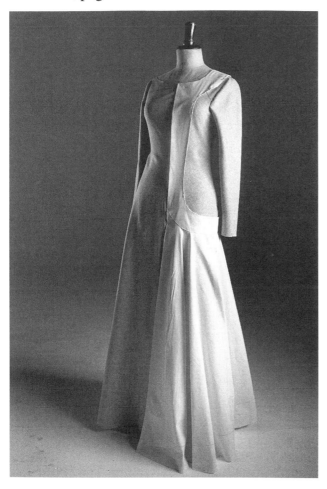

Plate 50. Toile of Lady Margaret Cobham surcoat.

Pattern Sheet 24. This pattern is for the type of surcoat with a separate fur plackard which is laid on to the skirt, similar to that of Jeanne de Bourbon (Figure 87), and the Strutt Ceremonial Surcoat (Figure 94.)

Cut the toile, making sure that you put in balance marks for the position of the side pieces and plackards, and then make up as follows:

1.   After the seams have been made up, put the top of the skirt on to a suitable band as an ordinary skirt, or, finish permanently by bind-ing over the top, to fit the hip.

2.   Make up the pieces of decoration for the sides between the front and back plackards by bagging out the top edge and turning and felling up the bottom, keeping them as flat as possible at the ends.

3.   Top stitch, over stitch or prick them to the top of the skirt, taking care not to either pull up or stretch the skirt top.

WATCH POINTS

When cutting a garment that will require facings, remember to cut them at the same time as the garment. This will save a great deal of time later.

When putting on the side pieces, put them on by placing them round the skirt not on flat, otherwise the skirt will become too small.

The plackard can be finished using the same method as described below.

4.   Position the plackard from the right side pinning or tacking it on to the skirt.

5.   From the wrong side, over stitch or prick the plackard on to the skirt. **WARNING:** If you are working with fur remember to remove all the pins.

6.   Finish by catching the top of the waist band with a long catch in the centre front or lightly herringbone across to the inside of the plackard.

If the surcoat and the bodice of the dress need to be held together as those of Lady Cobham and Queene Jeanne, 'Velcro'™ laid down the centre of the plackard should hold them together — hooks will slip undone and poppers/press fasteners will pull the underdress out of shape. The hip of the

Pattern Sheet No. 23.   Surcoat — Lady Cobham

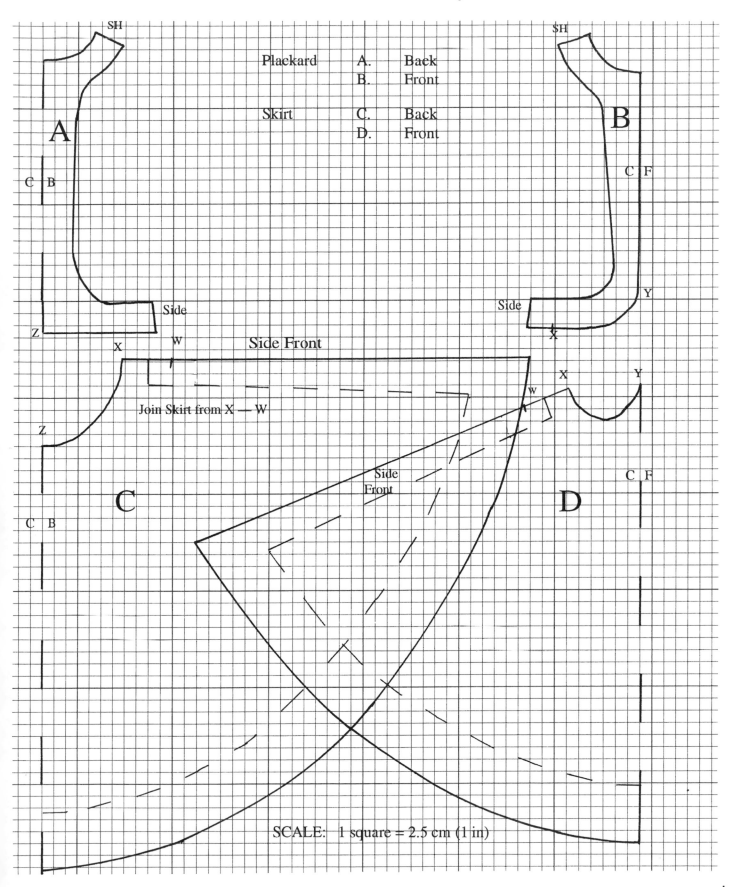

Plackard	A.	Back
	B.	Front
Skirt	C.	Back
	D.	Front

SCALE: 1 square = 2.5 cm (1 in)

Pattern Sheet No. 24.   Surcoat — Queen Jeanne de Bourbon

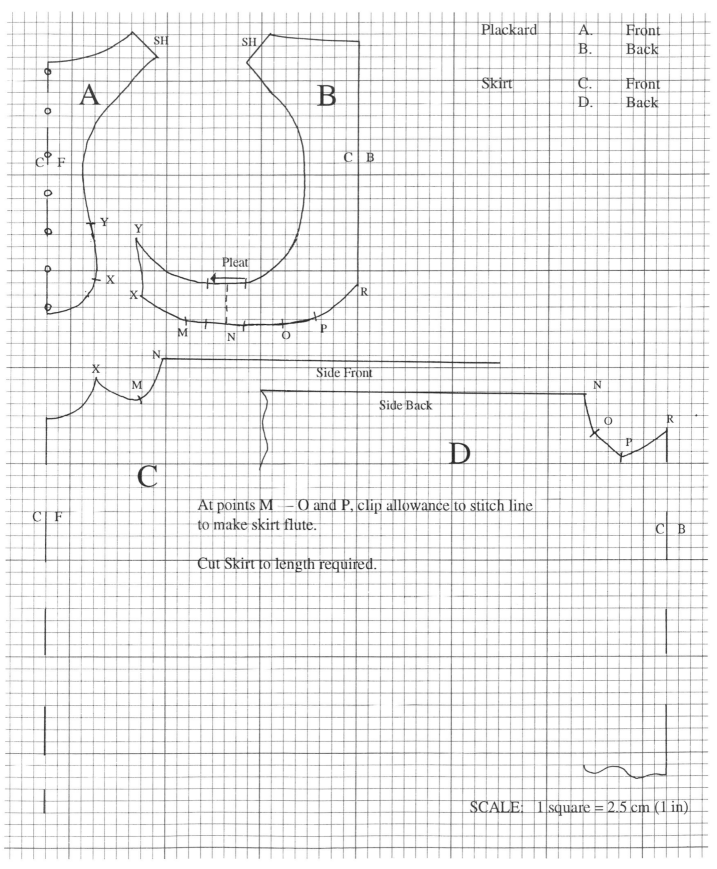

Plackard	A.	Front
	B.	Back
Skirt	C.	Front
	D.	Back

At points M — O and P, clip allowance to stitch line to make skirt flute.

Cut Skirt to length required.

SCALE: 1 square = 2.5 cm (1 in)

surcoat can be cut about 15 cm (6 in) larger on each side and fitted as Queene Jeanne of 1373/8 by folding it into a forward facing pleat. If it is possible to get into the garment with only one side made as a practical fastening the other side can be permanently stitched. A hook and bar with a popper behind can be used to hold the fastening secure.

METHOD 2. Cut on the Bias.

Pattern Sheet 25. The Salome Surcoat.

Pattern Sheet 26. Joseph Sequence Surcoat (Plate 51, 52.)

1. Cut two slashes out from the corner of a quarter circle of the toile fabric — the centre of which should be on the true bias — for about 15 cm (6 in.) Pin the centre of the fabric to the base of the neck at the centre front of the stand, continue pinning it at intervals, without stretching the fab-

ric, down the centre of the body of the stand.

2. Hold the fabric by its outer edge and swing it out and back once or twice enabling you to judge the amount of fabric that will be needed to create the correct amount of movement in the finished garment. When you gauge that you have the right amount of fabric across the front, pin the fabric to the hip of the stand.

About a quarter of a circle across the whole front is usually sufficient. Cut the back of the surcoat the same width across and then pin the side seams together. Try to keep the side seams on the same grain.

3. Mark out a rough neckline and armhole and then proceed as above. This sort of experiment will help to train your eye to the shape of the garment you are cutting, and the amount of fabric needed to create the correct amount of movement in the finished garment.

Plate 51. Front as Toile.

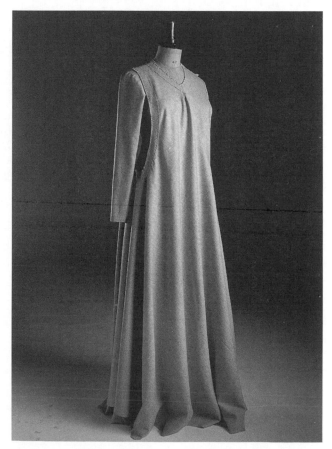

Plate 52. Finished Toile.

Pattern Sheet No. 25.   Surcoat 'Salome'

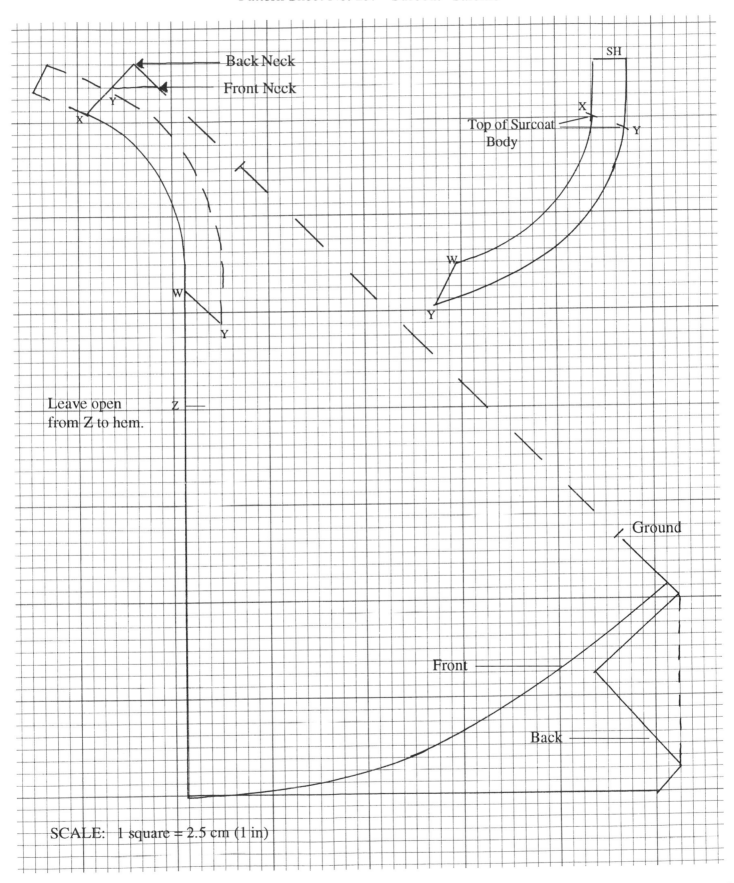

Back Neck

Front Neck

SH

X

Top of Surcoat
Body

Y

W

Y

W

Y

Leave open
from Z to hem.

z

Ground

Front

Back

SCALE: 1 square = 2.5 cm (1 in)

Pattern Sheet No. 26.   Surcoat 'The Joseph Sequence'

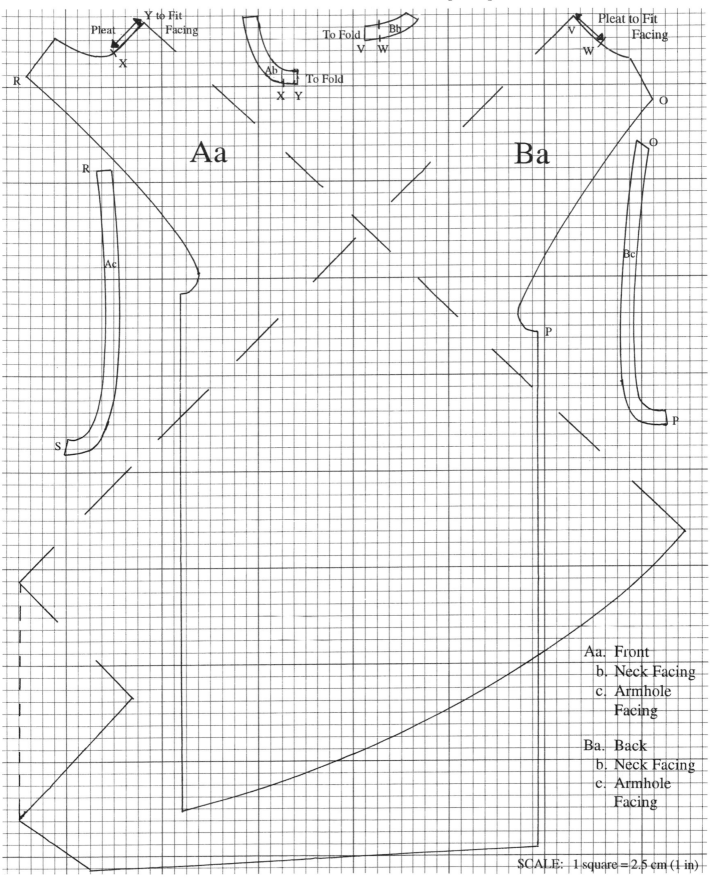

Pleat   Y to Fit Facing

X

To Fold   Bb

V   W

Ab   To Fold

X   Y

Pleat to Fit Facing

V

W

R

O

Aa

Ba

R

O

Ac

Bc

S

P

P

Aa. Front
   b. Neck Facing
   c. Armhole
      Facing

Ba. Back
   b. Neck Facing
   c. Armhole
      Facing

SCALE: 1 square = 2.5 cm (1 in)

FITTING

At the first fitting of the costume, fit the under dress or kirtle, deciding on its neckline, sleeve length, body fit, and width and length of skirt. If at all possible fit the surcoat as a toile rather than the real thing. This gives more freedom in the choice and changes of mind for the shapes of necklines etc., this often happens once it is seen over the under dress on the body, and will save both time and fabric, in the end.

After the fitting, make the toile into a pattern. If the garment is on the bias, a wheel piece will be needed on one side of the skirt, unless the fabric is very wide.

TO MAKE

Remember to hang all large pieces of the garment, if possible over night. If the main fabric is a firm weave the lining can be a regular coat lining, if not a mounting may be needed. When joining a wheel piece on to the body of a garment, the edges of both pieces must always be on the straight of the grain.

1. Cut the 'main' fabric and the facings for the neck and armholes. Also cut and 'mounting' and 'lining' fabrics, which may be required. Replacing the 'lining' where necessary with a more decorative fabric.

2. Mount the pieces and put a stay tape round the neck and armholes or machine round on the finish trace line. This will help to keep them from stretching.

Alternatively apply a strip of 'Staflex'™ or 'Vilene'™ fusible or if the fabric is very loose grained, put the fusible all through the plackard taking it about 5 cm (2 in) into the skirt.

3. Machine the side seams together, of both the main fabric and the lining separately, and the shoulders of the main body.

4. Face the neck and armholes — with shaped facings as a modern neck — and lightly herringbone down. (Piping could be used instead of facings or 'Hems Method 5' as used for hems, in Making a Basic Dress.)

5. Put the main body on the stand 'inside out', then put the lining over it, with the 'right side outwards', pin the seams together. Turn in the seam allowance of the lining to meet the edges at the armhole and the neck — pin and tack. Finish by adjusting the shoulder seams.

6. Fell round armholes and neck and across the shoulders of the lining to finish. Make sure that when you put the lining in, you do not distort the outside of the garment.

7. At the second fitting, if the skirt is designed to have a train or trail on the ground, get the hem length agreed by both the designer and the artist, or otherwise level it as the design.

8. After hanging the garment for as long as possible, finish the hem as explained in Making the Basic Dress, 'Hems Method 5' or as for cloaks below. Or, turn up the hem and fell the lining on to the edge.

WATCH POINTS

A sideless surcoat should be able to be put on without a front or back fastening if the armholes and necks are wide enough, but if it is necessary to have an opening for make-up and wig problems, make a very neat edge to edge fastening on the shoulder. Hanging loops on this type of garment are of great importance, put them on the sides of the skirt, do not expect the shoulders — unless the bodice is made of fur — to carry the weight of the skirt.

CLOAK (Plate 53, 54, and 55.)

The examples of the half circle cloak, are modelled on a half size stand. Although some commentators on costume seem convinced that the cloaks at this time are full circle, I think from observation it can be seen that half, or for a fuller effect, a three-quarter or a two third circular cloak is enough. Many cloaks are lined with fur which would make the full circle one extremely heavy (Figure 95.) Also too much fabric will not allow the cloak itself to drape into folds.

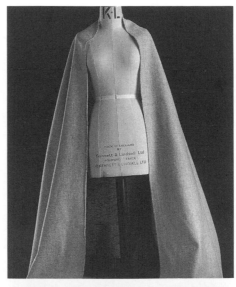

Plate 53. Front view of half circular cloak, on half size stand.

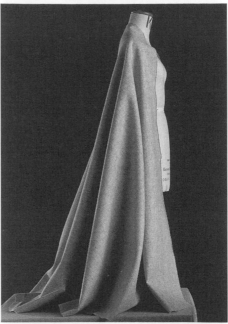

Plate 54. Side view, as above.

Figure 95. Fur lined cloak.

Plate 55. Rear view, as above.

A common feature of this period is that of cloaks being held in place by the wearer holding the fastening band or chain by the thumb and first finger (Figure 96.) This again points to a half circle cloak, as a three-quarter or full circle would sit more firmly on the shoulders.

Figure 96. Cloak fastening held by finger and thumb.

WATCH POINTS: When Cutting a Cloak

If the cloak needs to be cut with a train then a two third or three-quarter circle cut with a centre back seam will give a better line. Both sides of the cloak must be on the same grain.

The front edges must hang down dead straight, to achieve this, the fabric at the front edge, must be cut on the straight of the grain. The lining at this period always seems to come to the edge of the fabric all the way round, not stitched back from the edge as with a modern coat. The fullness of the half circle cloak can be increased by cutting the neck larger (see patterns) and gathering it into a band.

Lay the fabric out flat, on the table, if this is not large enough either put two or more tables together or use the floor. In the past, weather permitting, with really long cloaks I have had to resort to the lawn outside.

If its to be a half circle cloak, fold the fabric in half and cut both sides together.

To get the right measurement for the length of the cloak, place the tape measure at the side of the neck, take it to the outer edge of the shoulder and then down to the ground, add 7.5 cm (3 in) for the neck width, plus the depth of the hem.

To cut the curve of a large cloak pattern, you may need to join two tape measures. Put a drawing pin through the tape at the required length, and then into the table — if it is not an heirloom — otherwise get somebody else to hold it on to the fold of the fabric at the neck edge. Take the far end of the tape and run it round marking the fabric at intervals, making a smooth line.

***BEWARE:** make sure that the tape does not kink or drag where it is held at the neck end.*

If the cloak is to have a train, mark the halfway point between the front and the back. Now move this point 30 cm approx. (12 in) towards the back.

Next measure the required length down the centre
back and then draw a line making a smooth curve
between these two points.

If the cloak is three quarters or two thirds of a
circle, cut one side first, and then if the nap of the
fabric allows, lay the angled end of the second
piece into the angle left by the first piece.

If the cloak is to fit smoothly over the shoulders, you may need to put in darts or ease the
fabric slightly at the neck edge.

To get more fabric into a half circle cloak, cut
a larger neck hole and gather or pleat it to the neck
measurement required. Bind over the gathers to
finish the edge.

TO MAKE A CLOAK with no COLLAR

1. Join the centre back seam and wheel pieces
if any, of both the cloak and the lining.

2. Let it hang overnight.

3. Stitch a stay tape, round the neck line. If
the fabric is not of a firm quality it will also be
necessary to iron on a fusible facing both round
the neck and down the centre front edges.

4. Lay the cloak and the lining right sides
together. Machine round the neck and then down
both the centre front edges, starting from the neck
on both sides and finishing about 23 cm (9 in)
above the hem.

5. Clip the corners at the neck, trim, and snip
round the curve. Turn and press. Prick or edge
stitch the neck edge to keep it sharp.

6. If possible hang over night, over the shoulders of a stand. With the cloak still on the stand,
radiating from the neck, pin and then diagonal
tack the two layers together, stopping about 23 cm
(9 in) from the hem edge.

*Figure 97. Cloak with a tall collar, Uta, sculpture
Naumberg Cathedral.*

7. At the fitting, mark the length on ONE HALF OF THE CLOAK ONLY.

8. Trim back to about 5 cm (2 in), the hem allowance, on the side that has been fitted on both the lining and the main fabric. Fold the fitted side over onto the unfitted side, matching the grain lines, and trim to match.

9. Turn and press up the cloak hem and lightly herringbone up, lay the lining down, and fell to the edge of the cloak.

The hem could also be finished as in 'Making a Basic dress. Hems Method 5.

MAKING A CLOAK WITH A COLLAR

If the cloak has a collar like Uta's tall collar from a sculpture in Naumberg Cathedral, it will need to be stiffened with a good canvas to keep it in place (Figure 90.)

TO PUT THE COLLAR ONTO THE CLOAK

1. Put the outside of the collar on to the neck of the cloak.

2. Press the seam up into the collar and then bring the inside of the collar down, and without turning it in nick or ditch stitch it through on the seam line.

3. Fell the lining over the raw edge of the collar, positioning it over the seam line.

Uta holds the right side of her cloak in place from inside and the left side appears to be secured by a brooch.

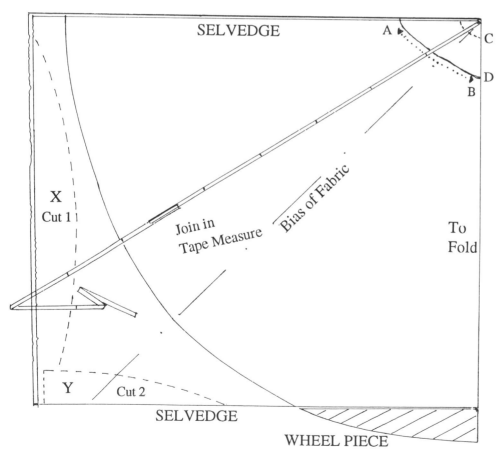

Figure 98.
A—B.   Gather to fit neck across the shoulder.
C.   Basic Neck Shaping.
D.   Neck shape to be flat at centre's Front and Back and gathered over shoulder.

X.   Wheel Piece cut in one piece.
Y.   Wheel Piece cut in two pieces with a join in the centre.
X & Y.   Alternative ways to cut the Wheel Piece.

This drawing is not to scale.

Pattern Sheet No. 27.   1/2 Circle Cloak with (A) No Neck Shape
(B) With Neck Shaping Gathered or Pleated across Shoulder from X — Z

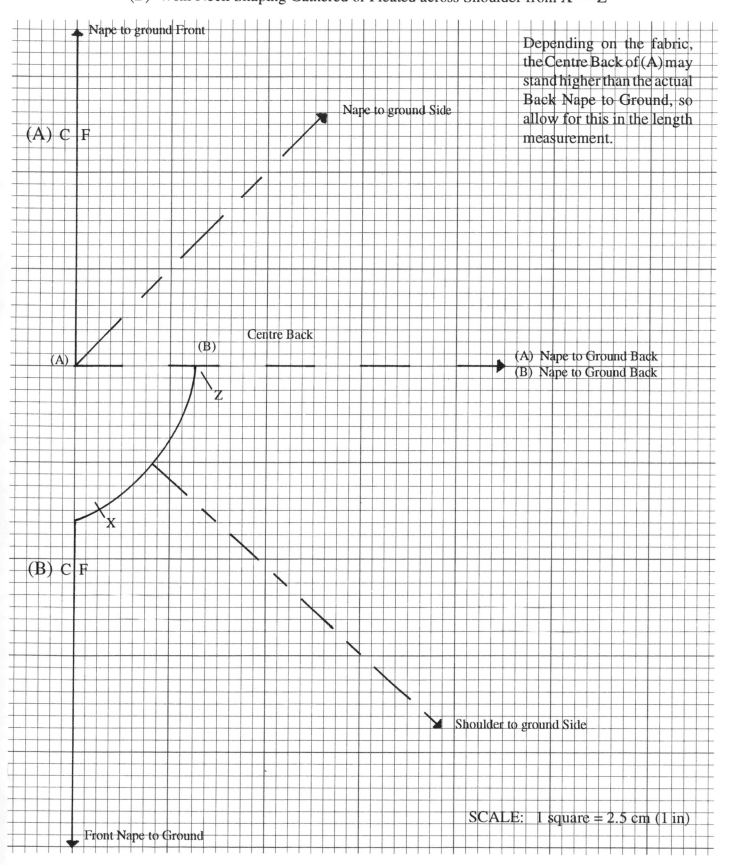

Nape to ground Front

Nape to ground Side

Depending on the fabric, the Centre Back of (A) may stand higher than the actual Back Nape to Ground, so allow for this in the length measurement.

(A) C F

Centre Back

(B)

Z

(A) Nape to Ground Back
(B) Nape to Ground Back

X

(B) C F

Shoulder to ground Side

SCALE: 1 square = 2.5 cm (1 in)

Front Nape to Ground

12. ITALIAN RENAISSANCE, 15th Century

This is one of the most attractive periods in which to dress many of Shakespeare's greatest plays, such as *'Othello'* and *'Romeo and Juliett,'* the story also used by Prokofiev for his ballet. The operas *'Otello'* and *'Simon Boccanegra'* by Verdi can also be set in this period. It is a designer's joy as it is such an inventive period. The men's costume can either be long and stately or short and frivolous, and the women's dress is also varied in shape and as with the Gothic costume has exotic headgear.

The fabrics are rich in texture and pattern, such as brocades and damasks, often with gold incorporated into the weave or embroidered on to the fabric. The textile designs are usually big and bold using pineapples and pomegranates and continuous branching foliate designs, many adapted in the nineteenth century by William Morris and in this century by Fortuny.

The styles vary not only with the passing of time, but from one Duchy or Republic to another. Each was ruled by a wealthy family such as the Medicis, Gonzagas or Sforzas, who appeared to wish to out do each other by the magnificence of their clothes. Luckily for us they had the means to employ artists, in some cases to design their clothes as well as record their wealth for posterity.

I shall deal in this chapter with specific garments rather than try to do a chronological look at a century in a country with such a wealth of variety and ideas.

This mosaic of Salome about *c*1350 from the baptistry of St Mark's in Venice (Figure 99) show her dancing with the head of St John the Baptist, for Herod, who is dressed as a Byzantine Emperor. It shows along with two other adjacent figures (not shown) the closeness in style to the lady from the Luttrell Psalter of 1340. Although they are different in feel — the subject of the psalter being more

Figure 99. Salome from St. Marks.

145

down to earth than that of the mosaic — the tippet, sleeves and the long straight gown are similar. The figures in the mosaics have split skirts edged with fur together with the wide band of gold decoration round the neck of the dress and the wrists of the underdress. This body-hugging dress is in red with gold spots and grey fur, and gold bands with white spots — presumably pearls — at the neck of the dress and sleeve ends of the blue underdress giving a Byzantine touch. This dress today could be made in a panne velvet embroidered with gold beads and pearls.

The first 15th century example is taken from the tomb of Ilaria del Carretto of 1406 (Figure 100.) The underdress has ample bagpipe sleeves ending in a deep cuff, with a second draped cuff turned back at the wrist. The over dress has a similar shape to that of the northern houppelande. The high collar is buttoned at the centre front, and the body of the dress can be seen to be split down to the waist. The hanging sleeves which open from below the shoulder, waterfall to the ground. The belt under the bust, controls the fullness of this voluminous dress. It could be made in, again a panne velvet, soft wool or silk, either plain or patterned.

The next dress is from the Casa Borromeo frescos in Milan (Figure 101) dating from the first half of the century. It is cut on a simple houppelande style with a widish belt under the bust and elaborately foliar shaped dagged sleeves; again it is very long and full. As the fabric in the drawing does not have any angles in its drapery the same soft draping fabric as above would work for this dress.

In this painting of 'The Birth of Venus', by Fra Carnevale from the Metropolitan Museum in New York, can be seen variations on a theme of the dress *c.*1467. It is a great favourite of mine as there are many female figures of both servants and ladies in the painting, showing the mix and match nature of the fashion of the time. All the women seem to be wearing the high waisted underdress

Figure 100. Ilariadel Carretto 1406.

146

which buttons or laces down the front, over which a variety of cloaks, coats and tabard like garments, often with sleeves of a different colour are worn.

the cartridge pleated skirt which is very long, it is split at the side to below knee level and finishs with a square ended train. A black belt placed about 5 cm (2 in) above the pleating of the skirt can be seen at the side, from it, is suspended a white handkerchief on a cord. The epaulette round the armhole which probably hides the attachment of the sleeve, seems to hold the tabard in place. The sleeve consists of a puff which reaches to just above the elbow, and continues as a tight sleeve to the wrist.

The second lady (Figure 103) wears a blue overdress, the skirt of which is attached to a high tabard type bodice which is split down the centre front. It must fasten under the arm at the

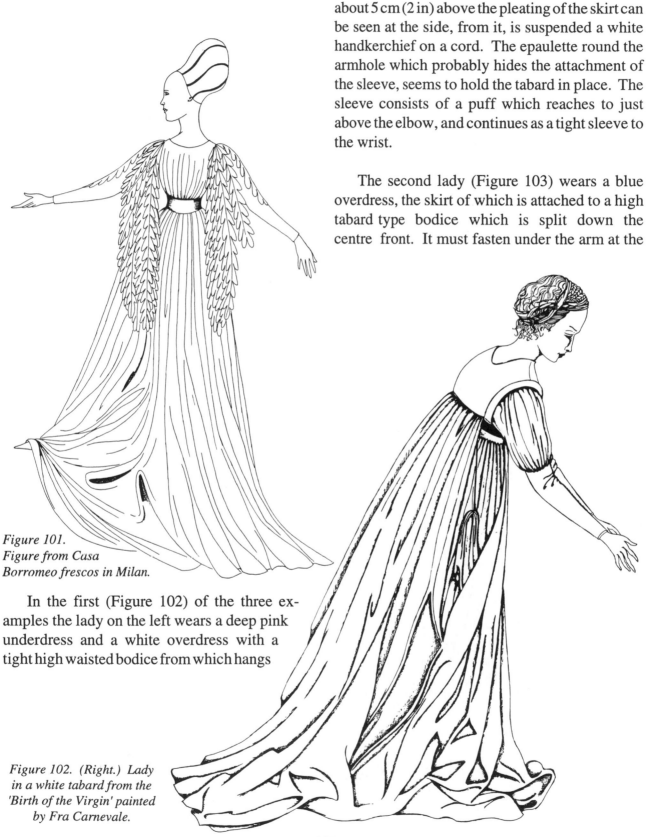

Figure 101.
Figure from Casa
Borromeo frescos in Milan.

In the first (Figure 102) of the three examples the lady on the left wears a deep pink underdress and a white overdress with a tight high waisted bodice from which hangs

Figure 102. (Right.) Lady
in a white tabard from the
'Birth of the Virgin' painted
by Fra Carnevale.

side in the same way as the white dress but the fastening is hidden by the hanging sleeves. The under skirt is green but the darker blue sleeves which are the same style as those of the first dress are attached to a white head or yoke. She also has a handkerchief between her fingers.

The third example (Figure 104), probably the

Figure 104. (Right.) Lady wearing a pink cloak.

garment that can be seen under the two over dresses above, has a mid-rib length bodice which is laced across the centre front, and a cartridge pleated skirt. Many of the other figures in the painting are wearing dresses of the same style. Over her head, she wear a pink cloak or shawl probably over a bun shaped headdress. The skirt, although it is well onto the ground, is not so long as the other two figures.

Figure 103.(Left.) The second Lady in a blue overdress.

The frescos *c.* 1470 of the Triumph of Minerva and the Triumph of Venus by Francesco del Cossa and Cosimo Tura in Ferrara, both show gatherings of people. The first is of young women variously weaving, spinning, cutting and working at an embroidery frame. The second shows young men and women chatting and wandering around just like an opera chorus. These frescos formed the basis for the chorus costumes of a production of *Simon Boccanegra* I worked on. By looking at the frescos various styles of neckline, sleeves and the methods of fastenings can be seen. This white dress (Figure 105) with a high waist is very similar to Figure 104, the fastening is at the front and could be laced (Figure 106) or buttoned. She wears a sage green apron with a darker border, which is probably pinned to the bodice as it has no visible strings. The sleeve is black and the chemise can be seen as a puff at the forearm.

There are two variations of the sleeve worn by the figures in these paintings and both are set well on to the shoulder. First a long tight sleeve with a small puffed head with an opening in the seam which is placed at the back of the lower arm

Figure 105. White dress with apron, 'Triumph of Minerva.'

Figure 106. Dress laced down the front.

showing the chemise. (Pattern Sheet 33, Sleeve 5.) The second is not split at the back but is cut longer and then ruched or pleated from the upper

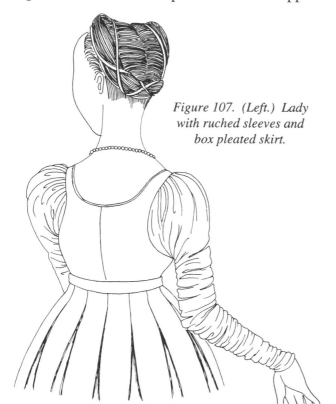

Figure 107. (Left.) Lady with ruched sleeves and box pleated skirt.

arm to the wrist (Figure 107.) This would look better if it was accordion or antique pleated before it was made up other wise this type of sleeve is apt to look like a bandage. The puffed head and setting of the sleeve will help the mobility of the upper arm, and the splits placed at the back on the lower arm will also give more freedom of movement.

One figure in the fresco is wearing a 'V' necked overdress with a wider sleeve which reaches to just below the elbow and is lined with a contrasting colour, coming from which is the ruched sleeve of the underdress (Figure 108.) Two of the examples also have hanging sleeves, Figure 110 is similar to the sleeve pattern on Pattern Sheet 32, Sleeve 3.

Of the three views of the backs of the bodices, two are 'U' shaped and one is a 'V'. This low back neck acts like a dart releasing the tension across the back of the bodice as in Figure 107.

The skirts in Figures 105, 106, 108, are cartridge pleated, and those in Figures 100 - 101 are cut through as a houpplande which allows a greater width at the hem while the amount of fabric at the waist is less than a straight skirt. But the back view from the 'Triumph of Venus' is box pleated (Figure 107), the pleats being stitched down for about 8 cm (3 in) from the waist. Organ pleats — a rounder, wider version of cartridge pleats, are often used in the theatre today but their construction makes it difficult to get enough fabric into the skirt — about 3 m (3 1/2 yds) are needed in the width of the skirt — to give enough movement at the hem. They are approached in the same way as cartridge pleating, but each pleat is stitched for at least 1 cm (1/2 in) along the waistband, the inside of the pleat therefore needing to be correspondingly deeper to take

Figure 108. Lady with 'V' neck etc.

up the width of the fabric, and to allow for the lesser number of pleats.

Figure 109. Rear view, a double sleeve.

Figure 110. Rear view of a turned back, hanging sleeve.

The next dress is from a painting of the Ferrarese school of the betrothal of 'Jason and Medea' (Figure 111.) It shows a white dress with sleeves and stomacher in red. This dress is the same style as the last but the skirt which is cut on the straight is made in a finer fabric giving it a slimmer line. It has a very high waist which is accentuated by a narrow black belt. The 'V' neck of the white is edged with a gold embroidered braid, as is the red stomacher. The red straight sleeves have no fullness in the head and are open from above the elbow to the wrist, but are caught together half way down the fore- arm allowing the chemise to be seen

Figure 111. (Right.) Lady in white from Jason and Medea.

151

as two puffs through the split. The underskirt appears to be of cloth of gold.

This lady from 'The Visitation' by Domenico Ghirlandaio *c.*1486-9 (Figure 112), from a fresco in Florence, shows a different style of dress. The waist is still slightly above the waist, which can be

Figure 113. A lady with moire bodice and partlet. Painted by Ghirlandaio.

Figure 112. (Left.) Lady wearing a tabard from 'The Visitation' by Ghirlandaio.

seen by looking at the other women in the picture (not Illustrated.) Both the under and over dresses are of beautiful brocades. The under dress is in burnt orange patterned with gold and green lattice. It can be seen through the side of the tabard as well as at the centre front, where it is probably laced across the chemise. The sleeve which is quite complicated is split on the lower arm above the wrist, at the elbow, and at the front half of the sleeve head. At the back of the upper arm the puffs are very regular and controlled, as are those on the outside of the arm which I think could be false.

The brocade of the overdress is of cloth of gold with white or silver birds, probably an heraldic device surrounded by an architectural design. The dress could be joined at the centre front from just below the waist to the ground or it could be open like a coat. It looks as if the front is controled at the side by a belt passing under the back panel which hangs straight from the shoulder to ground like a tabard. The hem is level with the ground at the front and dragging slightly at the back.

152

Figure 114. Chemise worn by Venus from 'Venus and Mars' by Botticelli.

Ghirlandaio depicts many of his women wearing variations of this style of dress and if faced with the task of making the period it would pay to find other examples of his paintings.

This painting of a Lady, *c.*1490 (Figure 113) also by Ghirlandaio, shows very clearly the detail of the front of a bodice which is in green moiré. It laces with a dark green lace through purpose made gold hooks across the front over the chemise which can also be seen through the gap at the front of the sleeve. The partlet, which is frequently seen worn by the ladies in the Holbein drawings at the beginning of the next century, fits very close to the body and seems to be attached to the lacing at the centre front.

The chemise worn by Venus in the painting by Botticelli of 'Mars and Venus' (Figure 114) is the embellishment of a simple undergarment as are those in his famous painting 'Spring'. When seen in conjunction with this Pisanello drawing (Figure 115) of a garment obviously meant as bust control

Figure 115. Pisanello drawing of a bra like chemise.

Figure 116.
Alegorical Figure
showing laced front
and sides, painted by
Cosimo Tura.

it becomes more clear as to how the underwear at this period worked.

From the National Gallery in London this allegorical figure of the late 1450's (Figure 116) by Cosimo Tura, wearing what I take to be the dress seen worn under, for example, the overdress from 'The Visitation' described above. The bodice, which is drawn tightly round the body by the lacing down the centre front and the sides, and the skirt which is cartridge pleated on to the bottom of the bodice is of dark green velvet. The sleeves are a rich red and gold brocade, and are cut in two pieces, a puff, which is cartridge pleated at both the head and the bottom, ends just above the elbow, where it is joined to the tight sleeve which ends at the wrist. From about 7.5 cm (3 in) below

the elbow the sleeve is split along the seam, the chemise being drawn through the gaps. The sleeve can be made as Sleeve 4, Pattern 33. The chemise can also be seen through the unfinished lacing of the skirt.

Also in London's National Gallery is a Virgin and Child painted in the same style. The bodice of this example is fastened with two buttons, and only the wrist of the sleeve can be seen, again fastening with buttons. This garment (not illustrated) appears to be in the same fabric as the sleeves of the one above. Of about the same date another painting in the Budapest Museum of Fine Arts of a similar type by Michele Pannonio (Figure 117) is of an underdress or kirtle which is cut straight through from shoulder to hem, again it is laced at the front and sides as far as the low hip, it has short set in sleeves, which are banded with gold on the edge as is the neck. The skirt is pulled up over the knee showing the the hem which is approximately 30 cm (12 in) deep faced on to a green moiré lining. She wears a chemise under the kirtle which has narrow sleeves ending in a shallow cuff, which can also be seen through the lacing and at the hem where it finishes just above the ankle. Both artists were employed by the d'Este family in Ferrara.

Figure 117. Alegorical figure showing Kirtle, laced front and sides, painted by Michele Pannonio.

PATTERNS FOR COSTUMES IN THIS CHAPTER

Pattern Sheet 10, the houppelande, 1400 to 1450 can be used as the basis for the garments in this chapter. The fabric is softer and the linings are not so heavy as the Northern European dresses, so that more width may be needed to get the right effect.

Pattern Sheet 28. (Plates 57, 58, 59) has both the dress and tabard for the 'Birth of Venus' by Fra Carnevale as well as the Medea bodice (Plate 56.) All the bodices will need mounting on drill or a good sheeting to give the firm smooth look. I have given the pattern for the front skirt, but the back could be cut in two pieces with a flared seam at the centre back, but try to keep the sides on the straight of grain.

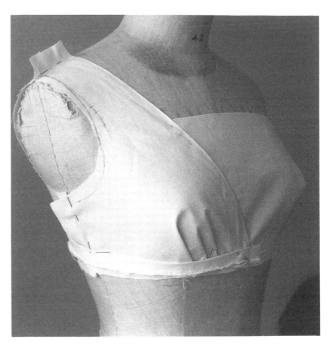

Plate 56. Toile of the Medea bodice and stomacher.

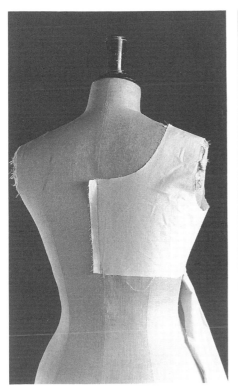

Plate 57. Toile of the back with skirt for White tabard.

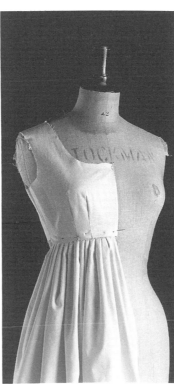

Plate 58. Toile of the bodice for under White tabard.

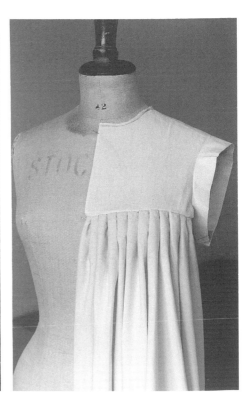

Plate 59. Toile of the front with skirt for whit tabard.

Pattern Sheet No. 28.   'The Birth of Venus' A and B — 'Medea' C.

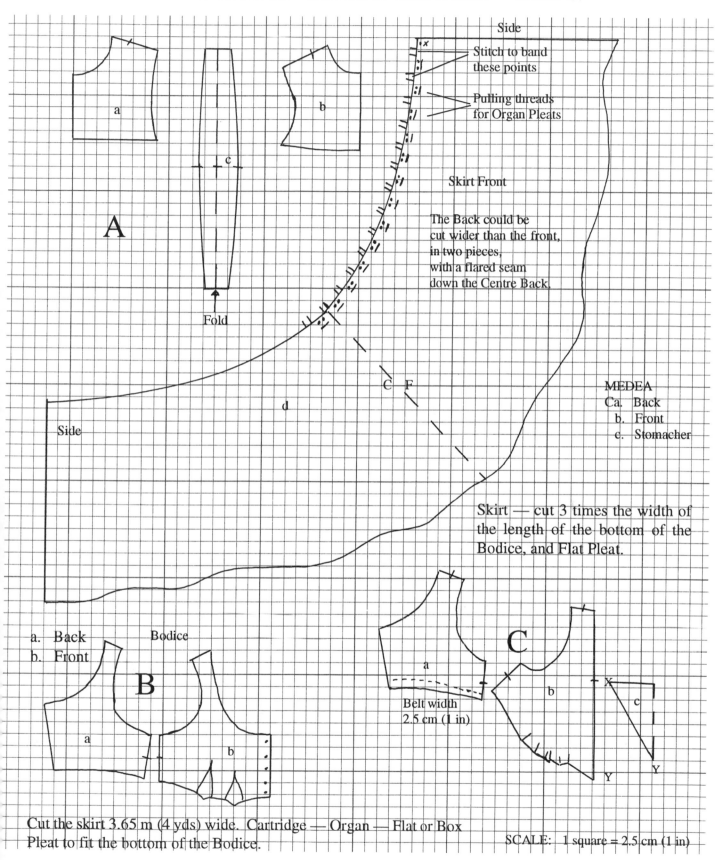

Side

Stitch to band
these points

Pulling threads
for Organ Pleats

Skirt Front

The Back could be
cut wider than the front,
in two pieces,
with a flared seam
down the Centre Back.

A

c

Fold

Side

d

C F

MEDEA
Ca. Back
  b. Front
  c. Stomacher

Skirt — cut 3 times the width of
the length of the bottom of the
Bodice, and Flat Pleat.

a. Back   Bodice
b. Front

B

a

b

C

a

Belt width
2.5 cm (1 in)

b

X

c

Y

Y

Cut the skirt 3.65 m (4 yds) wide. Cartridge — Organ — Flat or Box
Pleat to fit the bottom of the Bodice.

SCALE: 1 square = 2.5 cm (1 in)

Pattern Sheet 29. The Tabard for 'The Visitation' (Plate 60.) The fabric needs to be a stiff brocade otherwise it will need a firm mounting fabric. This garment is also fully lined.

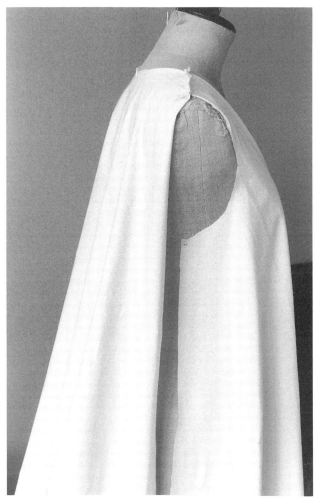

Plate 60. Toile of the Tabard for 'The visitation'.

Pattern Sheet 30. 'Venus' (The width of this garment is governed by the type of fabric used, and would need to be made wider rather than narrower. Ideally a very fine soft fabric which is opaque, such as a fine Swiss cotton lawn or voile; jap silk may work, depending on its quality, but it would need to be washed after it had been made up to take out the dressing. Otherwise chiffon could be used but it would need to be cut wider, be difficult to keep clean, and it would probably need a lining. The right quality of fine

fabrics to make this type of garment are very difficult to find.

Most of these patterns can be made up using the 'Making a Basic Dress' chapter. The bodices which are cut separately from the skirts, will need mounting and the skirts can be either cartridge pleated, box pleated or gathered as the design dictates. The large loose garments can be made as already described.

Plate 61. Toile of the chemise for 'Venus".

158

Pattern Sheet No. 29.   Tabard — 'The Visitation'

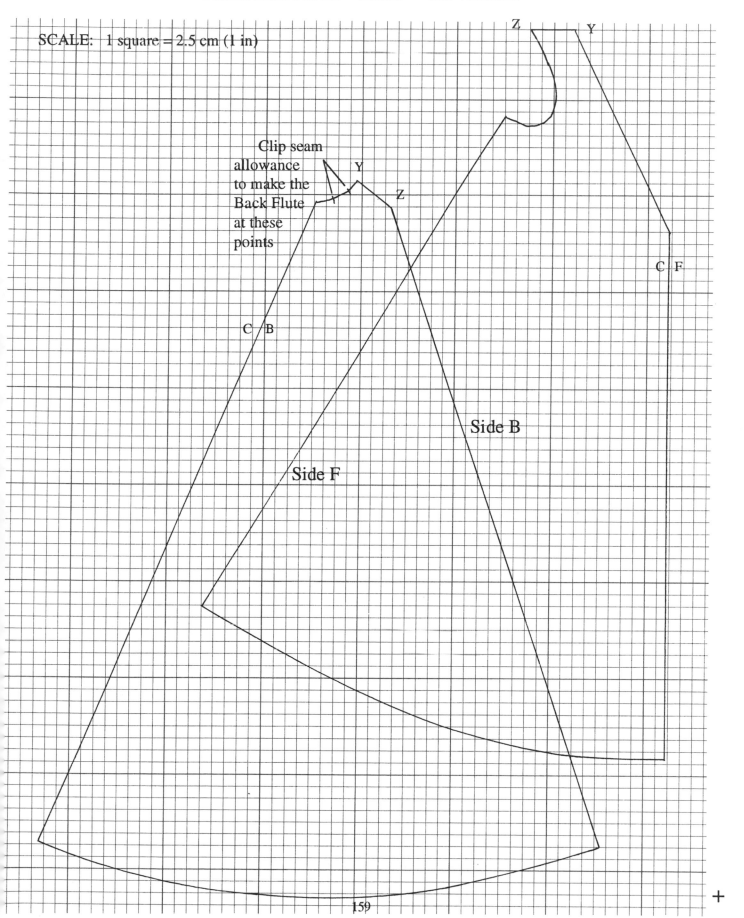

SCALE: 1 square = 2.5 cm (1 in)

Z   Y

Clip seam
allowance
to make the
Back Flute
at these
points

Y

Z

C F

C B

Side B

Side F

Pattern Sheet No. 30. 'Venus' Chemise

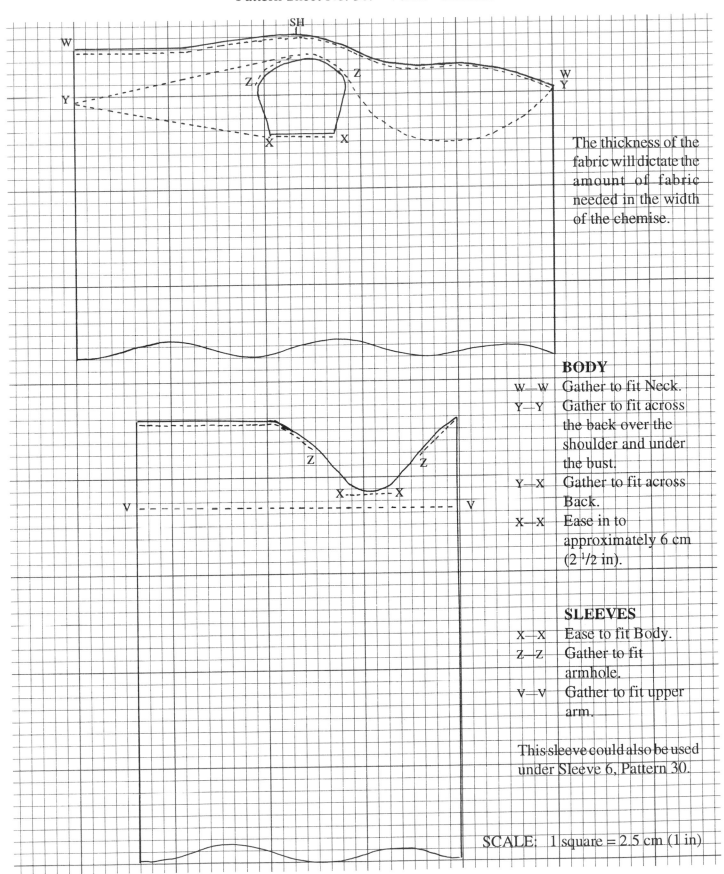

BODY

w—w	Gather to fit Neck.
Y—Y	Gather to fit across the back over the shoulder and under the bust.
Y—X	Gather to fit across Back.
X—X	Ease in to approximately 6 cm (2 1/2 in).

SLEEVES

X—X	Ease to fit Body.
z—z	Gather to fit armhole.
v—v	Gather to fit upper arm.

This sleeve could also be used under Sleeve 6, Pattern 30.

The thickness of the fabric will dictate the amount of fabric needed in the width of the chemise.

SCALE: 1 square = 2.5 cm (1 in)

SLEEVES

As with Gothic dress, the sleeves make an important contribution to the variety in the styles. In addition to sleeves seen on women's dress, I have included patterns that are of interesting design, which only seem to occur in men's fashion. Cutting and making costume for men, is, with a little adjustment, the same as when making them for women.

The hanging sleeve patterns from the 1400 to 1450 chapter can be used as a base for sleeves for the houppelande style of hanging sleeve.

SLEEVE 1. (Figure 118.)

Dagged sleeves such as those in Figure 101 were used by John Gunter in a production of *'Simone Boccanegra'* at Glyndebourne, but in his design he lengthened the foliar shaped dagged strips to ground length. The dress was made in grey panné velvet, which when it was under stage lighting it looked silver, and was printed with a gold and bronze Italianate design.

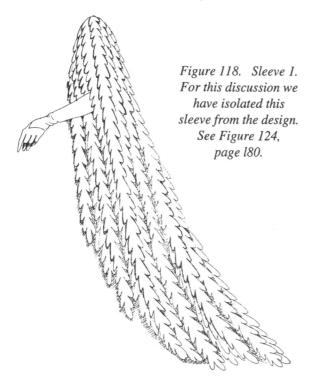

Figure 118. Sleeve 1. For this discussion we have isolated this sleeve from the design. See Figure 124, page 180.

TO CUT AND MAKE

The basic hanging sleeve Pattern Sheet 15, Sleeve Da, page 96, can be adapted for this sleeve, by reshaping the bottom, and adding 2 or 3 extra strips to get the balance right. When this type of sleeve is cut into strips it becomes less substantial

Divide the pattern into 7.5 cm (3 in) wide strips, or the width that you require for the design of the dags. This type of sleeve is very fragile and liable to be stepped on and so needs to be strongly made.

1. Cut a template for the dags sufficiently long to enable it to be overlapped when drawing out the strips (Plate 62.)

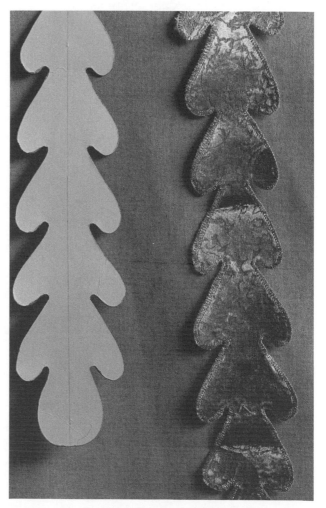

Plate 62. Template and finished length of dagging.

2. Cut the strips plus at least 1.5 cm (^{1}/2 in.) allowance on both outside edges. Iron these on to a double sided fusible, (this is usually backed onto paper) strip off the paper and iron this on to a suitable decorative lining.

3. Draw the pattern of the dags on to the lining side and straight stitch round the line.

4. On a close zig-zag stitch, which is suitable for buttonholes, machine round the pattern — the width of the stitch will depend on the fraying quality of the fabric, and the side from which you work will depend on the machine stitch. A metallic thread can be used to give extra glitz. The instruction book of the machine usually gives guidance whether it is better to use metallic threads on the top of the machine or on the bobbin.

5. Cut round the dag design as close as possible to the stitch.

6. When the strips are finished lay them on to the original sleeve pattern and cut them to their final lengths. It is a good idea to number each strip to avoid problems when putting the sleeve together.

7. Cut a soft nylon net base, the shape of the pattern, which will reach as far as the elbow.

8. Lay out the strips lining side up, in the right order, flat on to a table.

9. Lay the net on top and catch the strips on to it through the centres with a running stitch.

10. Machine the strips to the net round the head.

The net will help to control the strips at the top of the sleeve without destroying the lightness of the design, and allows the long lengths, from the elbow to the ground, to move freely. Treat it from now on as an ordinary solid sleeve.

TO FINISH THE HEAD OF THE SLEEVE
Depending on the thickness of the fabric either gather the head and put it straight into the armhole, or cartridge pleat it.

To cartridge pleat the sleeve into the armhole:

A. Bind over the head of the sleeve and the armhole of the garment with a narrow binding, first cut down the allowance to the finished line.

B. Cartridge pleat the head by organizing the pleats as explained in 'Sewing Techniques'. Although the amount of pleating is small compared to a skirt, still put two threads through to hold them in place.

Do not tie or cut off the threads until the sleeve is finished.

C. Pin the bodice and sleeve together, arranging the pleats round the head where required, check the position on the stand before you finally over stitch the pleating into the bound armhole. This type of sleeve is very time consuming and therefore very expensive to make, and needs to be used for an important character.

Any sleeve that is made with fullness in the head can be treated the same way.

Pattern Sheet 31. Figure 119, Sleeve 2.

Sleeve 2. is a man's sleeve from 'The Adoration of the Magi' by Domenico Veneziano *c.* 1440. The fabric at the head and the wrist hole of the sleeve would need to be cartridge pleated to get the amount of fabric needed for this effect into the armhole and wrist. (See Sleeve 1. To Finish the Head A— C above.)

1. Cut the sleeve in both fabric and a lining. The slit at the front of the arm can be bound or piped with a contrasting fabric and the lining felled in, or alternatively it could be bagged out as follows.

Pattern Sheet No. 31.   Sleeve 2 — 'The Adoration of the Magi'

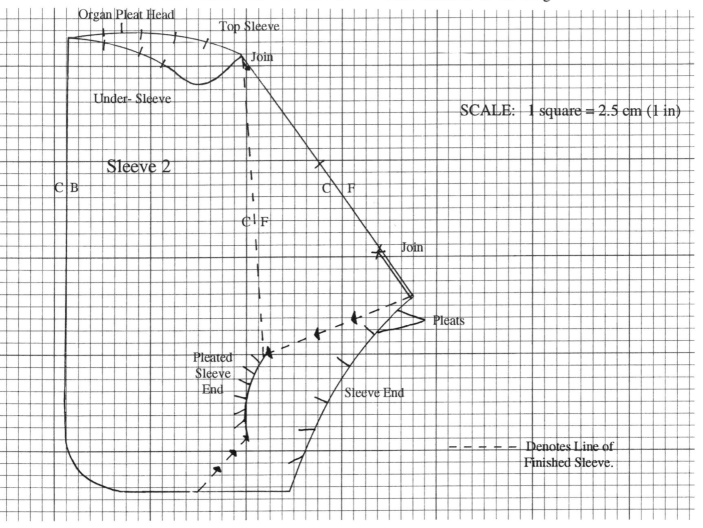

Organ Pleat Head

Top Sleeve

Join

Under- Sleeve

SCALE: 1 square = 2.5 cm (1 in)

Sleeve 2

C B

C F

C F

Join

Pleats

Pleated
Sleeve
End

Sleeve End

— — — — — Denotes Line of
Finished Sleeve.

Figure 119. This very grand 'bagpipe' sleeve is worn by one of the three kings in the painting of 'The Adoration of the Magi' by Domenico Veneziano. The whole costume, as befits the character, is very grand. The over-garment is made in a brocade with a deep decorative hem. The sleeves appear to be lined with fur and bound with a plain fabric at the wrist. The over-garment is worn over a dark velvet doublet, the sleeves of which appear to be similar to the under-sleeve 4a, Figure 121, in this chapter. The bagpipe sleeve could be made fuller than the pattern by adding in more fabric to both the under and top part of the sleeve pattern, and then re-shaping the head. The sloping front seam should stay the same.

2. Bag out the main fabric with the lining down the front split, from the armhole to the bottom of the split on both sides. Press the seam open and clip the allowance as far as the seam at the end of the split and pin them together.

To join the bottom of the front seam.

3. Machine the main fabric together, from the wrist to the bottom of the split — across the seam—then continue up the lining. Trim, press the seams open and turn the lining into the sleeve, tack the wrist ends of the sleeve together with the raw edges of the sleeve and lining seams facing each other, and edge stitch.

4. Make a padded rouleau to fit the wrist. Cartridge pleat the wrist end of the sleeve and stitch it to the padded roll. To set the sleeve into the head, bind the armhole of the bodice and the head of the sleeve, and continue as for 'To Finish the Head of the Sleeve A—C' Sleeve 1, in this chapter.

5. Alternatively, if the fabrics are fine enough it may be possible to gather both the head of the sleeve and the wrist, and put the sleeve into the armhole as a modern sleeve, and bind over the gathers at the wrist.

Pattern Sheet 32. Sleeve 3. Figure 120 A & B.

Sleeve 3, in the painting of a very fashionable young man by Domenico de Bartolo *c.*1443, the sleeves are very spectacular. Made in what appears to be a figured velvet lined with fur. The sleeve (a) as seen from the back is thrown or caught up onto the left shoulder and (b) the sleeve hanging down is the same length as his tunic. The sleeve in Figure 110 is a similar style and could be made in the same way. If the sleeve was to be lined with fur, presumable fake, find the thinnest one possible.

1. Join the seams of both fabric and lining.

2. Tack, machine and then bind the heads together.

3. The head of the sleeve can be finished as for Sleeve' 1 in this chapter 'To Finish the Head of the sleeve A — C.' A small padded roll may be needed to lift the pleating into the right shape.

4. Level the bottom of the sleeve by pinning the pleating at the head of the sleeve into the armhole of the garment, and pad the shoulder of the stand to simulate an arm. Level the bottom of the sleeve and finish as applicable to the design.

WATCH POINTS

If more fullness is needed in the under arm of the sleeve, or it is difficult to get rid of the fullness, put a forward facing flat pleat into the underarm of the sleeve. All these sleeves need to be set well on to the shoulder, and the cartridge pleating should then give the sleeve head the desired lift. If the head needs more lift put a small pad under the pleats to help it.

A.   B.

Figure 120. Sleeve 3.

Pattern Sheet No. 32.   Sleeve 3 — 'A Fashionable Young Man'

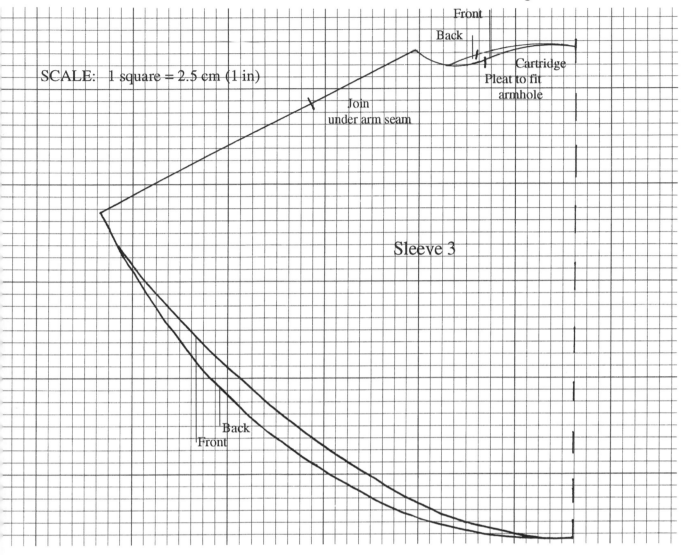

SCALE: 1 square = 2.5 cm (1 in)

Front

Back

Cartridge
Pleat to fit
armhole

Join
under arm seam

Sleeve 3

Back
Front

The sleeve of the cream and gold figured velvet or brocade of this very extravagant costume, is lined with fur, with a fur band round the bottom edge on the outside. It is worn pleated onto the shoulder, on his left, and worn down as a cape on his right side. The tight sleeve of the doublet with the frilled linen visible at the wrist, is orange in colour. Fur during the medieval period is often depicted as squares or shield shapes indicating the size of the animal pelts used. The drawing of the cloak, Figure 95, page 139, is another example.

PATTERN SHEET 33. Sleeve 4 a and b, Figure 121.

This double sleeve is from a painting by Piero della Francesca of 1452-66 and is similar in shape to those in (Figures 103 & 109.)

Cut the linings for the tight sleeve using — Sleeve C. Pattern Sheet 6 — from the Toile Chapter — in a firm cotton, such as cotton sateen, and for the short puff (4a) from this pattern sheet, cut in a suitable light weight stiffening such as net to support the fabric.

Cut the main fabric for the under sleeve, the puff and the tight sleeve. The tight part of the sleeve need only be covered where it can be seen.

Also cut the hanging sleeves (4b) in fabric and lining with an interlining if necessary.

TO MAKE the inner sleeve (4).

1. Bag out the fabric with the lining for the lower part of the tight sleeve — the part that is to be left open — and turn and press.

2. Tack the fabric and lining of the tight sleeve together at the wrist and machine across above the elbow. This is to hold the fabrics together and provide a firm line at the place where the puff sleeve is to be attached.

3. Mount the puff sleeve fabrics together, DO NOT MAKE UP THE SEAM, pleat the head of the sleeve to fit the armhole from * (asterisk) to * (asterisk), and across the bottom to fit the machine line on the tight sleeve.

4. Gather up the bottom of the puff evenly, then with the right sides facing each other, pin the bottom of the puff on to the machine line above the elbow of the tight sleeve. Tack and then machine starting and stopping 2 cm (^{3}/4 in.) from the outside edges.

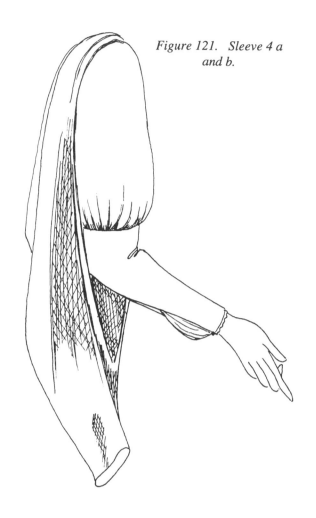

Figure 121. Sleeve 4 a and b.

5. Now stitch together the seam of the puff and press.

6. Pin the seam of the tight sleeve together, forcing the puff inside. Machine stitch the tight sleeve seam from the underarm to the elbow.

7. Press all seams, and turn the sleeve.

8. Pull up the gathering threads and arrange the fullness round the head, the fullest part being between * to * at the top of the sleeve.

9. Tack and then machine the heads of the puff and under sleeve together.

10. Finish the wrist and fastenings after fitting.

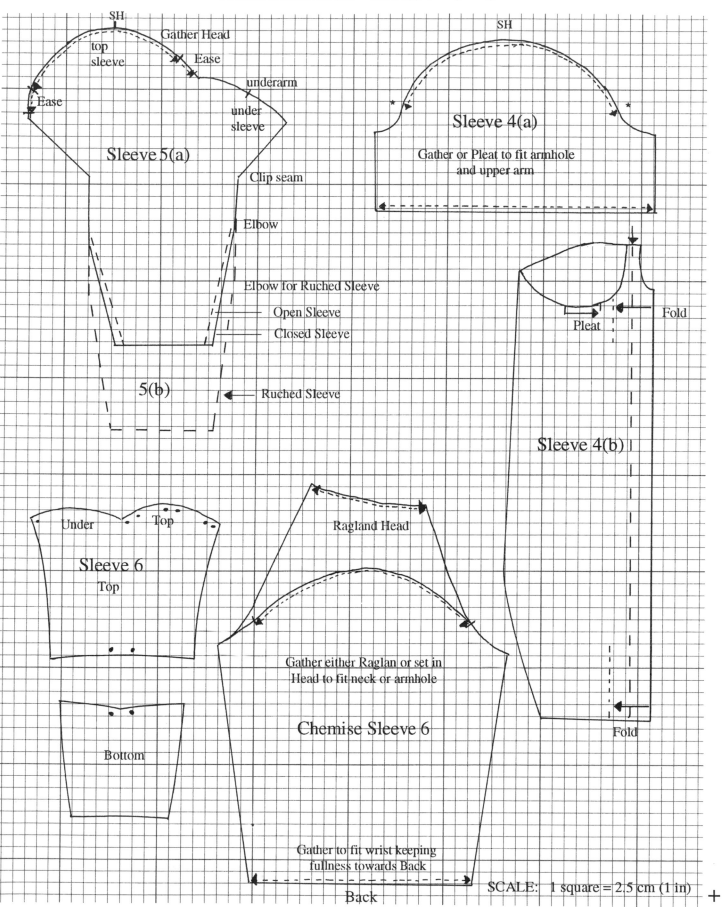

SH

top
sleeve

Gather Head

Ease

Ease

underarm

under
sleeve

Sleeve 5(a)

Clip seam

SH

Sleeve 4(a)

Gather or Pleat to fit armhole
and upper arm

Elbow

Fold

Elbow for Ruched Sleeve

Open Sleeve

Pleat

Closed Sleeve

5(b)

Ruched Sleeve

Sleeve 4(b)

Under

Top

Sleeve 6

Top

Ragland Head

Fold

Gather either Raglan or set in
Head to fit neck or armhole

Bottom

Chemise Sleeve 6

Gather to fit wrist keeping
fullness towards Back

Back

SCALE: 1 square = 2.5 cm (1 in)

11. Set into the armhole of the underbodice.

Make-up the hanging sleeve in a similar way to Sleeve 2 and set it into the over dress.

There are a number of ways to put two sleeves into one armhole to make it appear that there are two garments.

First make up both sleeves:
Method 1. Set the outer sleeve into the over garment as usual, and then bind the inner sleeve, and hand stitch into the armhole.

Method 2. Put the inner sleeve into the armhole and then lay the finished head of the outer sleeve inside out — round the armhole and whip it as near to the inner sleeve/bodice seam as possible. Pull the whipped in sleeve, back over the inner sleeve.

Method 3. Lay the outer sleeve flat on to the bodice and cover with a decoration or an epaulette.

Method 4. Put the outer sleeve into the main garment. Make an under bodice and stitch the inner sleeves into this. This is often the most satisfactory way.

Pattern Sheet 33. Sleeve 5 is to be used for sleeves in Figures 105-106 and can be adapted, by cutting it longer, for that in Figure 107.

Depending on the thickness of the fabric chosen for this sleeve it may need to be mounted on to an interlining, or if suitable, the lining which faces the open bottom half of the sleeve from the elbow to wrist, can be carried on up to the head and used as a mounting in the top half of the sleeve.

1. Bag out the bottom half of the sleeve to the elbow with a lining. If the sleeve is mounted, the lining can be cut off and felled down on to it. If the lining is used as a mounting, clip both lining and main fabric and either:

a. Stitch up the rest of the seam from the elbow to the underarm with all layers tacked together, (four layers in all), or,

b. Machine the main fabric as far as the elbow, machine backwards and forwards at the seam to reinforce it and then continue up the lining.

2. Clip at the angle on the upper part of the sleeve, (this creates a built in puff, and the underarm shape creates a built in gusset) and press the seam open.

3. Tack the main sleeve fabric and lining together at the head.

4. Put in gathering threads or cartridge pleat the head of the sleeve, as indicated on the pattern.

The sleeve is now ready to put into the armhole.

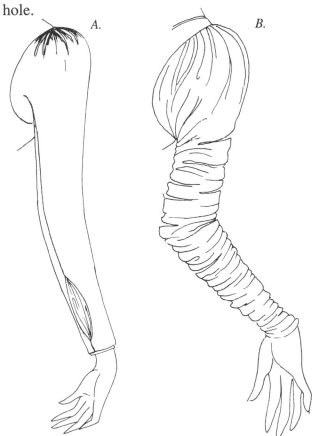

Figure 122. Sleeve 5. (A) The sleeve is cut with built-in puff and gusset (see Figure 105). (B) Ruched sleeve is cut longer, then pleated across the arm and then mounted onto a net lining (see Figure 107).

The sleeve from elbow to wrist can be caught together as the design with ties or decorative brooches or buttons.

Pattern Sheet 33. Sleeve 6

The other type of sleeve frequently seen in Italian paintings, are the tight sleeves through

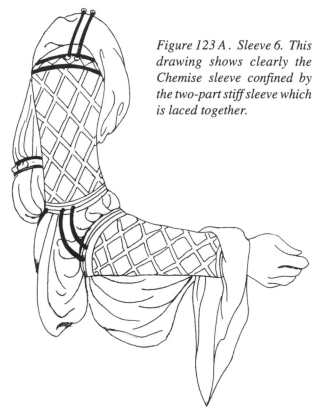

Figure 123 A. Sleeve 6. This drawing shows clearly the Chemise sleeve confined by the two-part stiff sleeve which is laced together.

which the chemise is pulled into puffs, as part of the decoration and which is illustrated in these drawings taken from various paintings.

TO MAKE THE SOLID PART OF THE SLEEVE

Bag out the separate pieces of the sleeve on three sides then turn in, bind or pipe the open end. Or, for a decorative effect 'bind over' all the way round the pieces in a contrasting fabric. The various sections can be attached together with eyelet holes and ties. The fabric for the most solid parts of the sleeve needs to be quite stiff so inter-

line them with canvas or vilene to get a crisp finish.

WATCH POINTS

1. Stitch elastic from one section to another behind the holes to support the ties.

2. Some puffs, such as those in the centre of the Sleeve on Figure 112, can be put on to the surface. Make a tube about 10 cm (2 in) wide when finished, cutting the fabric on the bias, make a small hole with a sharp pair of scissors or a stiletto where you want the puff to end, then gather the fabric into a bunch and — with great difficulty — force it through the small hole and catch it to the inside lining. I can guarantee the struggle will be worth it. What ever fabric is used for the puffs, to keep them fresh and puffy line them with a fine nylon net or tullé. By making a hole in the fabric and pushing through the puff there will be no messy finish at the ends on the right side of the sleeve fabric.

3. Always try to decorate the fabric before the sleeve is made up. See Sleeve 9.

4. Chemise sleeves that are to be pulled through tight oversleeves need to be worked out very carefully, concentrating the fullness were it is needed, usually towards the back, so that it can be pulled through easily.

5. If a separate chemise is not being worn, make a whole sleeve and stitch it into the head of the bodice and then fix the puffs if necessary by small diagonal tacks lightly round the gaps.

6. Look at the paintings of Titian to see how full chemises can be.

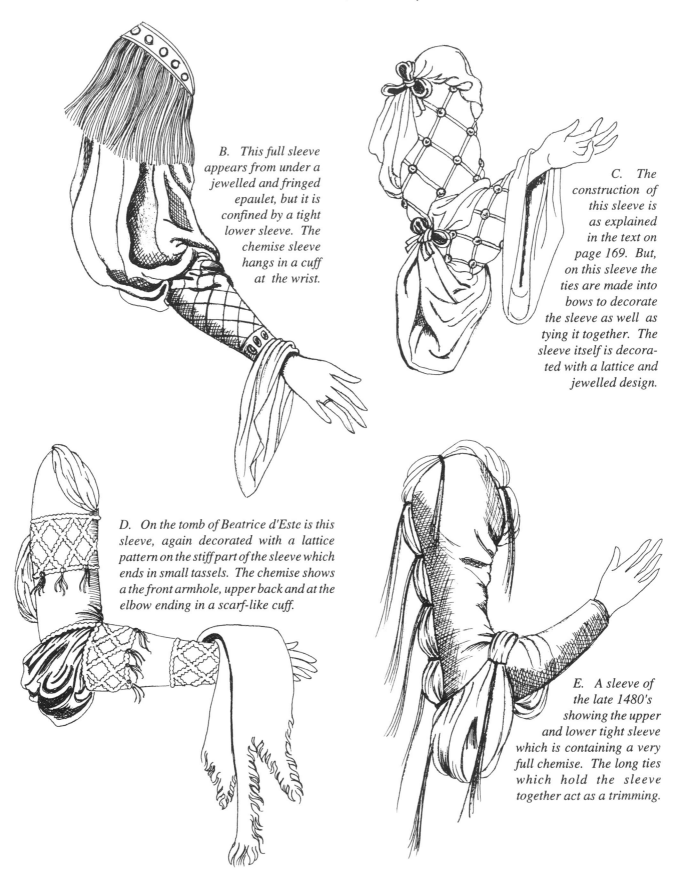

B. *This full sleeve appears from under a jewelled and fringed epaulet, but it is confined by a tight lower sleeve. The chemise sleeve hangs in a cuff at the wrist.*

C. *The construction of this sleeve is as explained in the text on page 169. But, on this sleeve the ties are made into bows to decorate the sleeve as well as tying it together. The sleeve itself is decorated with a lattice and jewelled design.*

D. *On the tomb of Beatrice d'Este is this sleeve, again decorated with a lattice pattern on the stiff part of the sleeve which ends in small tassels. The chemise shows a the front armhole, upper back and at the elbow ending in a scarf-like cuff.*

E. *A sleeve of the late 1480's showing the upper and lower tight sleeve which is containing a very full chemise. The long ties which hold the sleeve together act as a trimming.*

Figure 123. B, C, D, E. Variations on Sleeve 6. Pattern Sheet 33.

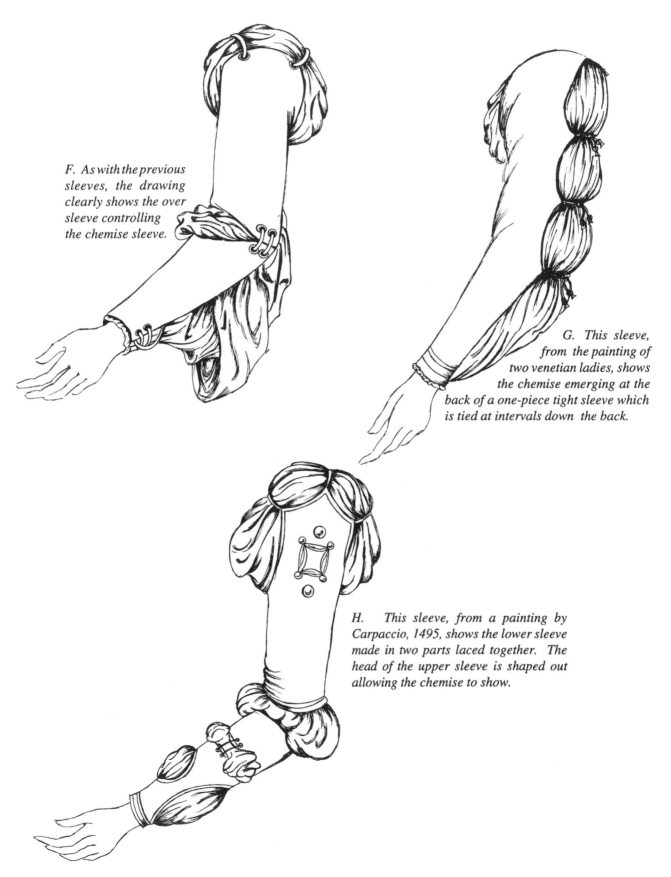

F. As with the previous sleeves, the drawing clearly shows the over sleeve controlling the chemise sleeve.

G. This sleeve, from the painting of two venetian ladies, shows the chemise emerging at the back of a one-piece tight sleeve which is tied at intervals down the back.

H. This sleeve, from a painting by Carpaccio, 1495, shows the lower sleeve made in two parts laced together. The head of the upper sleeve is shaped out allowing the chemise to show.

Figure 123. F, G, H. Variations on sleeve 6, Pattern Sheet 33.

Plate 63. This photograph shows four of the ball dresses made for the girls of the corps de ballet in the ball scene of the Kenneth MacMillan production of 'Romeo and Juliet,' designed by Nicholas Geordiardis for the New York City Ballet. They were made by three ex-students of my London College of Fashion one year course on 'Cut and Construction of Costume.' They are worn by students from the college 'Fashion Model Course,' and are in various stages of making. The costumes were made in panné velvet which was over-printed in a darker colour, in an Italian renaissance type design. The colourings were shades of greens, golds and russets, printed in darker shades of browns and greens. That on the left, without sleeves, is in orange printed in a rusty-brown, and sage green printed in a medium brown. That on the right, without its neckline decoration, is gold, also printed in a rusty-brown, but with a much more dense pattern than the first. Others in the group were printed in very dark brown and shades of green. (See Design 6, for more detail.)

PART THREE

13. INTERPRETATION OF COSTUME DESIGNS

For many years I worked as a freelance costumier, and made costumes for, among other managements B.B.C. Television, mainly for the drama department. Among the designers I worked for regularly, was John Bloomfield. I always enjoyed working for John, as, although on the whole he was faithful to the period of the piece he was designing, he approached it in an original way. From the many costumes I made for him I have chosen five. From the world of theatre Nicholas Georgiadis has allowed me to use one of his designs and John Gunter gave permission for Kathryn to copy one of his designs. They all fall into the period roughly covered by this book and show different aspects and interpretations of medieval dress.

Plate 65.

Design 1. 'Macbeth' by Shakespeare. Janet Suzman as Lady Macbeth. Designed by John Bloomfield, July 1970.

This costume was designed for impact, rather than accuracy of period. The under dress was cut as the sleepwalking and both costumes had tightly fitting sleeves, cut on the bias. It was made in a fine wool and with a hook and a bar back fastening. It was sprayed with a black pattern after it was partially made up. The dress was always worn covered, first by a surcoat and latter by this rather grand robe.

The large red, black and gold robe was made of a cotton rep with velvet facings, yoke and sleeves.

Plate 64.

173

Plate 66.

The sleeves were appliqueed from the cuff end with a flame like furnishing brocade. The body of the robe was sprayed with a large black motif which was 'embroidered' in latex which was painted gold. Today this type of decoration could be done with a glue gun which would make the finished costume lighter in weight. The red velvet facings and yoke were treated in the same way. The sleeve which was cut to fit smoothly into the armhole widened out into a bell shape which was pleated into a braid and jewelled cuff.

The body of the robe was cut in four panels, similiar in shape to Pattern Sheet 29 'The Visitation'; the back panels being cut wider and joined to the front down the sides, were pleated on to a yoke to give the back, which ended in a train, more fullness. The yoke was covered by the head-dress and hair.

Design 2. Janet Suzman. Lady Macbeth sleepwalking, as above.

The night-dress for the sleepwalking scene, was made in a fine slub silk noile which was printed once the centres, front and back, seams had been finished. It is cut on the bias using Pattern Sheet 2, and the front lacing was stiffened in a similiar way as that described in 'Fastenings E Method (b) in Sewing Techniques. The neck was stiffened slightly by six rows of machining narrower than half the foot of the sewing machine apart see: Sewing Techniques - 'Foot's Width Away'.

Plate 67.

Design 3. Macbeth Opera by Verdi. 'Profile Grace Bunbry'. Ms. Bunbry as Lady Macbeth, sleepwalking scene, August 1974.

For this programme Miss Bunbry broke her journey in London to do fittings on her way from America to Italy. She sang six arias for the programme, and all six costumes had to be fitted in toile form so that I could have them finished when she returned to do the programme three months later.

Miss Bunbry arrived on Saturday morning for rehearsal in the studio and most of the excerpts from the operas were recorded on Sunday. John Bloomfields designs were very clever, all six costumes could be finished or altered very quickly. They either glided over the body as this dress does, had an underbust or hip line 'waist' or a corset type of over bodice which was laced. To level the hems

I left surplus fabric at the waist which allowed me too either lift or drop the hem line.

On this design for Lady Macbeth the join was under the belt at the hip, enabling me to finish the time consuming long hem and the front fastening, made as in Fastening E. Lacing Method (a) in Sewing Techniques. After fitting my only jobs were to machine in the sleeves and the hip seam and long catch the belt to the dress.

The fabric for this design was a grey rayon jersey; because it would stretch, I used Pattern Sheet 1. It was cut across at the hip were it could be hidden by the belt, which was made in a dark red ottoman, cut on the bias. The weight of the skirt and the sleeve ends—a detail reminiscent of those on the dress from the Winchester Bible (Figure 36)— helped the jersey to mould to the body.

Plate 68.

Plate 69.

Plate 70.

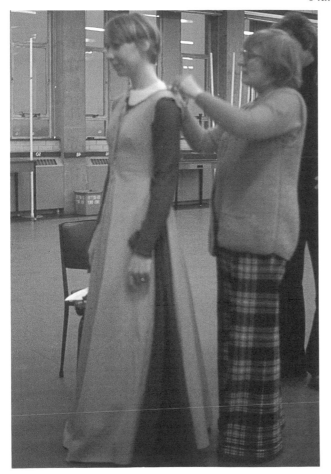

Plate 71.

Design 4. 'The Peasant's Revolt', Plates 70, 71, Episode 11, for a series called 'Churchill's People' which was based on Winston Churchill's 'History of the English Speaking People'. These very real figures are very like those in the Lutrell Psalter. The costumes were made from dyed cotton, noiles and wools. The cut is very straight forward, patterns that can be used are those from the Toile chapter or from Middle Ages to 1400 for the 'T-shaped' underdress; and 'Cyclas', Pattern 20 for the overdress.

Design 5. 'A Wilderness of Roses' (Plate 72.) The design shows Margaret Paston played by Gemma Jones in another Episode from 'Churchills People'. The costume consists of a houppelande lined, or in this case edged with fur. The belt high under the bust holds the dress in place. The sleeves of the under dress can be seen through the split in the over sleeve.

Although the houppelande should be cut through, the bodice in the design was in a plain mid-olive velveteen, but the skirt was made of about four different shades worked in random stripes to make up the width required. The skirt was cartridge pleated on to a band, and the bodice was made up separately and stabbed onto the same band, the join being covered by the belt. The sleeves had no fullness at the head, but at the wrist, the front over the thumb was flat, the bulk of the fabric being cartridge pleated at the back into the cuff. When it was finished the whole dress was sprayed to blend the various colours of velvet together.

Plate 72.

Design 6. 'Romeo and Juliet' designed by Nicholas Georgiardis (Plate 73); Corp de Ballet, Ball Lady, for Kenneth MacMillan's production in New York. Mr Georgiardis's designs are always interesting, and the productions when on the stage look wonderful. The design is very reminiscent of Pisanello, with its long slim line and high elaborate headdress. This is one of four designs made in russets, golds and greens for the big ball

scene in the Prokofiev ballet. The costumes for the ballet were made in England by the army of free-lance makers who regularly make costumes for productions that go all over the world. This particular set of ball dresses were made by three of my ex-students.

The fabric for this design was light olive green panné velvet over printed with brown or dark green with an Italian Renaissance design. The skirt and overskirt were both cut as three-quarter circles, with the waist cut larger than the midriff waist measurement and then gathered on to a fitted 'waist' band. The sleeves were amazing. The organza puff sleeve, at the top, is eased into the armhole and gathered into the tight band on the upper arm. The large bagpipe sleeves took 2 meters (2$\frac{1}{4}$ yards) of fabric each. (See Pattern 34.) It was gathered along the fold which fitted along the top of the arm, and at both ends to fit the

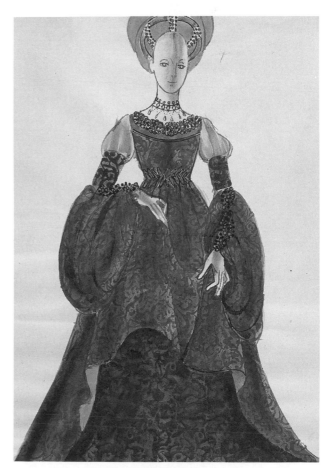

Plate 73.

upper sleeve and cuff. The whole of this sleeve was mounted onto an inner sleeve to help it to stay in place. The bodice was quite stiff, with a slightly high waist.

All the jewellery was made by a prop maker, the belt being made up of gold leaves, the beads on the sleeves and neck were loose ropes of black, gold beads and pearls mounted on to net which was stitched permanently to the dress. The necklace was made on a souffle yoke which was probably stitched into the neck of the dress when they had been fitted in New York. They wore large headdresses familiar in the early 15th century, which would have accentuated the height and stately appearance of the dancers. I only saw the costumes as in the photograph (Plates 63, 74) partially finished on fashion models at the London College of Fashion, but as a group they were by any standards, as most of Niko's costumes are, spectacular. I have to thank Carol Hersee for the loan of the pattern and information about the making of the costume.

Plate 74.

Pattern Sheet No. 34. 'Romeo and Juliet' Corp de Ballet Ball Dress, Designed by Nichola Georgiadis

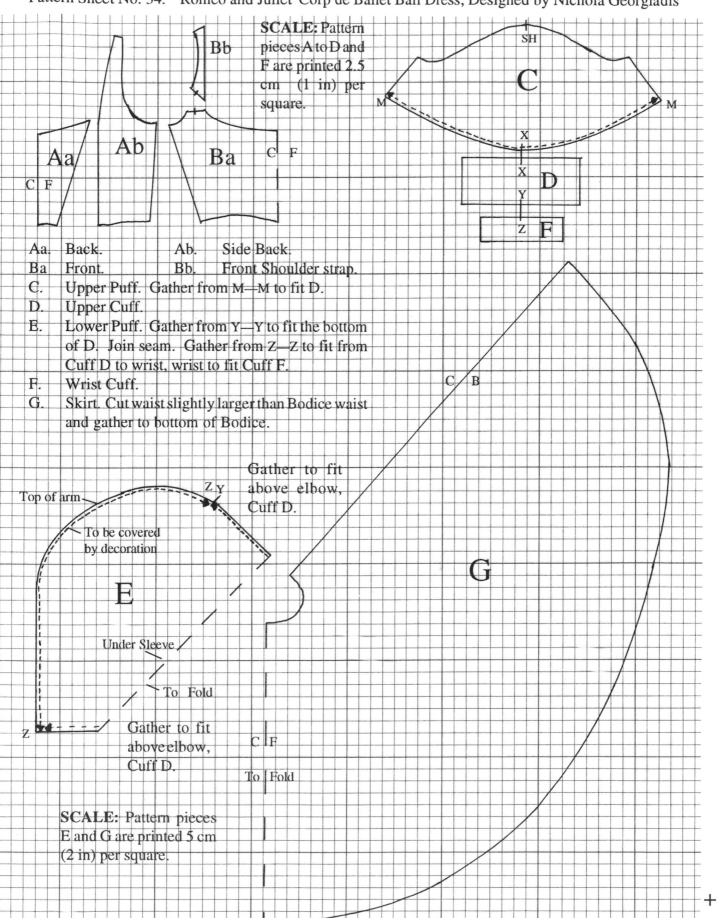

SCALE: Pattern pieces A to D and F are printed 2.5 cm (1 in) per square.

Aa. Back.   Ab.   Side Back.
Ba   Front.   Bb.   Front Shoulder strap.
C.   Upper Puff. Gather from M—M to fit D.
D.   Upper Cuff.
E.   Lower Puff. Gather from Y—Y to fit the bottom of D. Join seam. Gather from Z—Z to fit from Cuff D to wrist, wrist to fit Cuff F.
F.   Wrist Cuff.
G.   Skirt. Cut waist slightly larger than Bodice waist and gather to bottom of Bodice.

Gather to fit above elbow, Cuff D.

Top of arm
To be covered by decoration

Under Sleeve

To Fold

Gather to fit above elbow, Cuff D.

To Fold

SCALE: Pattern pieces E and G are printed 5 cm (2 in) per square.

Design 7. 'Simon Boccanegra' Act III by Verdi, designed by John Gunter for the 1986 Glyndebourne season. Maria Boccanegra was sung by Carol Vaness. The drawing is an interpretation by Kathryn (Figure 124) from the original design. The dress was grey panné velvet which under the stage light became silver, it was printed with a gold and bronze pattern. The panné was mounted on to a cotton lawn and was cut through from shoulder to hem like a Houppelande. The pleats at the 'waist' were caught on to an inside belt. The tight inside sleeves were put into the armhole, and long foliate hanging sleeves were bound and cartridge pleated on to a band and then stitched on to the shoulder of the dress. The back of the dress was on the ground by about 51 cm (20 in.) The making of the long foliate sleeve is described in 'Italian Renaissance' Sleeve 1, the longest lengths being 1.77 m (70 in) and the shortest at the front 61 cm (24 in.)

The fabric for both the 'Romeo and Juliet' and the 'Boccanegra' costume were printed by Demetra at 'Classic Fabric Design' DHA Lighting London, as is the close-up of the sample in the Fabrics chapter.

All these designs presented a challenge, but when successful, costumes such as these are very rewarding to make.

A.

B.

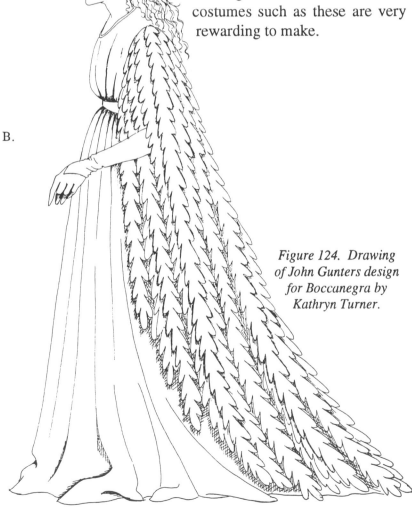

Figure 124. Drawing of John Gunters design for Boccanegra by Kathryn Turner.

Plate 75. A. Front View. B. Back view.

14. SOURCE INDEX

		Fig	Page	Patt
BRASSES:				
Gown, Joan de la Pole, 1380.	Chrishal, Essex	46	66	1, 2
Gown, Lady Harsick. 1384	Southacre, Norfolk	48	68	1, 2
Houpplande, Lora de Saint Quintin, 1397	Brandsburton Yorks	50	77	11
Houpplande with Peter Pan collar. 1410–20.		51	78	11
Stiff bodice and Circular skirt. 1490	West Harling, Norfolk	72	107	19
Surcoat, Lady Margaret Cobham. 1375	Cobham, Kent	84	125	23
Surcoat, Lady Walksokne. 1349	Kings Lynn, Norfolk.	83	124	
ENAMEL:				
Lady from Enamel on a box lid. 1380	The British Museum	49	69	
FRESCOS and PAINTINGS:				
Alegorical Figures:				
Tura, Cosimo. Lacing front.	The National Gallery, London	116	154	
Pannonio, Michele. Lacing side and front	Museum of Fine Arts, Budapest	117	155	
Botticelli	The National Gallery, London			
Mars and Venus		114	153	30
Brussels Master of the Joseph Sequence				
Surcoat	The Cloisters, New York	91	128	26
Carnevale, Fra.				
'The Birth of the Virgin' , *Three examples*	The Metropolitan Museum, N.Y	102- 4	147- 8	28
Christus, Petros.				
Lady in Brocade dress, 1449, 'St, Eligius'	Metropolitan Museum of Art, N.Y	65	102	11
Donnatrix	National Gallery of Washington, D.C.	66	103	17c
Eyck, Jan van				
The Arnolfini Marriage	The National Gallery , London	pl. 29	80	12
Ferrarese School				
The Bethroval of Jason and Media.	Staatliche Museen, Berlin-Dahlem	111	151	28
Ghirlandio, Domenico:				
The Visitation	Santa Maria Novella, Florence	112	152	29
Moire bodice and Partlet	Metropolitan Museum, Florence	113	152	
Birth of john the Baptist. Side lacing bodice	Santa Maria Novella, Florence	77	119	
Lady with foliat sleeves	Palazzo Borromeo Frescos, Mila	101	147	
Lady at Prayer, Jeanne de Bourbon-Vendome	North Carolina Museum of Art	75	110	
Marmion Simon				
The Devil, from the Altar of Saint Bertin	Staatliche Museen, Berlin-Dahlem	67	103	17A
Memling, Hans				
The Donne Triptch	The National Gallery, London	pl. 41	105	17B
Master of Saint Bartholomew Altar Piece				
St. Peter and Dorothy	The National Gallery, London	78	120	
Queene Jeane, 1373–8	Louvre, Paris	85	125	
Francesco del Cossa, Triumph of Minerva.	Palazzo Schifanoia, Ferrara			
White dress with apron		105	149	
V-neck bodice with double sleeve		108	150	
Bodice lacing down front		106	149	

		Fig	Page	Patt
Francesco del Cossa, Triumph of Venus.	Palazzo Schifanoia, Ferrara	107		28
Dress with ruched sleeves and box pleated skirt.				Bod.
Dress with Two piece puff and hanging sleeves.		109	151	33sl
				4a,b
van der Weyden, Rodier				
The Braque Triptych, Kirtle Front	The Louvre, Paris	61	84	13
The Descent from the Cross, Kirtle Side	Prado, Madrid	60	84	13
The Altarpiece of the Seven Sacraments'1445, Kirtle back	The Royal Museum of Fine Arts Antwerp	62	85	13
The Altarpiece of the Seven Sacraments. 1445 Houppelande with shawl collar	The Royal Museum of Fine Arts., Antwerp	58	82	
Young Woman 1435	Kaiser Friedrich Museum, Berlin	59	83	
Magdalan Reading	National Gallery, London	57	82	11
The Bladelin Alterpiece, Chemise	Staatliche Museen, Berlin-Dahlem	79	121	21
Salome, Surcoat	Staatliche Museen, Berlin-Îahlem	88-9	127	25
Zavattari Brothers. Story of Queen Teodolinda V-back neck with hanging sleeves folded back over shoulder.	Monza, Duomo	110	151	32Sl

MANUSCRIPTS

		Fig	Page	Patt
Book of Hours of Marie d'Harcourt,Duchess of Guelders	Staatsbibliothek, Berlin-Dahlem	53	79	11
Book of Old Testament Illustrations, 1260				
Cloak with fur lining	Pierpont Morgan, Library New York	95	139	27
Cyclas		82	124	22
Kirtle with narrow sleeves and pouched bodice		40	62	8c
Early 16th century manuscript				
Lady writing letter	Bibliothéque Nationale, Paris	71	107	
Side view showing dress tucked up over belt				
English Apocalyps 13th century	Conway Library. Courtald Institute of	37,39	61	
3 figures from a copy of an Apocalypse	Art	9		8
Fortune, 1460's	BibliothéqueRoyale, Brussels	68	104	17
Franco-Flemish Manuscript executed by Loyset Liedet	Bibliothéque Royale, Brussels			
Queen Dowager Gown of Houppelande type, 1448		64	101	11
Square sided Surcoat 1448		90	128	
Lacing kirtle down front, an amalgam of two sources		76	118	
Roman de la Rose 1490	The Bodleian Library, Oxford England			
The Hours of Anne de Beaujou	Pierpont Morgan Library, N.Y.			
Master of Rene of Anjou	Österreichische National Bibliothek,			
Lady receiving a book	Vienna	69	105	17
Les Trés Riches Heures du Duc de Berry 1412	Chantilly, Muséum Condé.	52	78	11
Luttrell Psalter, 1340	British Library. London			
Lady Luttrell		41	63	22
Lady from,		42	63	10
Back view of an acrobat		43	64	

		Fig	Page	Patt
Strutt "Habits and customs of the People of England"	Victoria & Albert Museum, London			
Kirtle with purse hanging from belt		86	126	1-4
Loose overdress showing kirtle with pocketed hem.		44	65	4
Surcoat with skirt tucked into side armhole with kirtle with pocket hem		80	123	
Surcoat showing it lifted at front with kirtle with pocket hem		81	123	
Pocketing sleeve		34	59	
Surcoat lifted at the back		92	129	
Side view short Surcoat		93	129	
Ceremonial wide back		94	129	
Wisdom unfinished figure from the Winchester Bible.	Winchester Cathedral, England	36	60	2

MOSAIC

		Fig	Page	Patt
Salome	St. Marks, Venice	99	145	

PAINTINGS see Frescos and Paintings.

SCULPTURES

		Fig	Page	Patt
Amsterdam Bronzes.	Rijkesmuseum, Amsterdam, Nederlands	54,56	81	11
A Queen from a sculpture with extra sleeve, 1150	Chartres Cathedral	35	60	
Cloak Holding fastening with finger and thumb.	Strassburg Cathedral	96	140	27
Iaria del Carretto. 1406 Tomb Sculpture.	Lucca Cathedral	100	146	11
Uta with collar, 1249-80.	Naumburg Cathedral	97	141	27
Weeper Edward III, 1377.	Tomb of Edward III, Westminister Abbey, London	45	66	2,3 / 1,2
Ceremonial Surcoat Queen Jeanne de Bourbon	Poitiers, Palais de Justice	87	126	24

TAPESTRY and TEXTILES

		Fig	Page	Patt
Bodice, The Triumphs of Petrach – Chastity over Love	Victoria and Albert Museum, London	73,74	108-9	20
Dress with buttons down sides and sleeve and with skirt turned back to waist	l'Hotel de Cluny, Paris.	70	106	
Cuff, first half of 13th century.	Museum of London	pl.25	67	

DRAWINGS FROM TEXTILES AND PAINTINGS (Misc.)

		Fig	Page	Patt
1400 to 1450 sleeves.	Various sources.	63	92,93	14-16
Italian Renaissance sleeves.	Various Sources.	123	169-71	31-33
Early 16th Century Sleeve.	Museum of London	31	46	6d
Cuff Drawing of Inside.	Museum of London	47	67	
Pisanello drawing of bra like chemise.	Drawn from a copy in the Witt Library, Courtland Institute of Art.	115	153	

15. BIBLIOGRAPHY

Book List for the Period. *The following books are available and among the most reliable and accurate   sources of information for quick reference.*

Backhouse, Janet. *The Luttrell Psalter.* 1989.
- - - *Books of Hours.* 1985.
- - - *The Becket Leaves.* 1988.
The British Library.
- - - *The Illuminated Manuscript*
1979. John Murray.

Birbari, Elizabeth. *Dress in Italian Painting.* 1975. John Murray Publishing.

Boucher, Franois. *A History of Costume in the West.* 1967. Thames and Hudson.

Crowfoot, Elizabeth; Pritchard, Frances; Staniland, Kay. *Medieval Finds from Excavations in London (4). Textiles and Clothing, c1150 - c1450.* 1992. Museum of London.

Cunnington, C. Willett and Phillis. *Hand Book of English Mediaeval Costume.* 1952. Faber and Faber Ltd..

Davenport, Millia. *A Book of Costume.* 1948. Crown Publishers.

Donovan, Claire. *The Winchester Bible.* 1993. The British Library/Winchester Cathedral.

Fairholt, F. W. *Costume in England,* (2 vols, Octavo.) 1885. George Bell and Sons, 4th edition 1909.

* Geijer, Agnes; Franen, Anne Marie and Nockert, Dr. Margaretta. *The Golden Gown of Queen Margareta in Uppsalla Cathedral.* 1985. Revised 1994. Kungl, Vitterhets; Historie Och Antikvitets Akademien.

Harthan, John. *Books of Hours.* 1977. Thames & Hudson Ltd.

Herald, Jacqueline. *Renaissance Dress in Italy 1400-1500.* This is part of *The History of Dress Series.* 1981. Bell and Hyman.

Houston, Mary. *Medieval Costume in England and France.* 1939. A & C Black.

Kelly, Frances M. and Schwabe, Rudolph. *A Short History of Costume and Armour 1066 - 1800.* 1931. B. T. Batsford Ltd.

Koler, Carl. *A History of Costume.* 1928. David McKay Company.

Mayo, Janet. *A History of Ecclesiastical Dress.* 1984. B. T. Batsford.

* Nockert, Dr. Margaret. *Bockstensmannen och hans Drakt (The bocksten man and his costume.)* 1985. Stiftsen Hallands lansmuseer, Halmstad och Varberg.

Planché, J. R. *Cyclopaedia and Dictionary of Costume. (2 vols. quarto.) 1873.*

Scott, Margaret, *Late Gothic Europe 1400 - 1500.* This is part of *'The History of Dress Series'.* 1980. Mills and Boon.

Stainland, Kay. *Medieval Craftsmen: Embroiderers.* 1991. British Museum Press.

Strutt, Joseph. *Dress and Habits of the People of England.* (2 vols.) 1793. Reprinted, 1970. Tabard Press.

Specialist books on subjects such as Monumental Brasses, Effigies, Stained Glass, Illuminated Manuscripts and Paintings. General publications on European Art and History will give a good background to the period.

* *Both Swedish books, above, have a summary in English and captions to the photographs are in both English and Sweedish.*

16. INDEX

	Page		Page
Aiglet	11	Inlays	20
Antique Pleating	31	Lining	20
Baby Hemmer	11	Measurement Chart	28
Bag or Turn out	11	Mounting	21
Balance marks	11	Mounting and Making a Bodice	50
Basting (see Flat tacking.)	18	Museum of London. 13th Century Cuff.	67
Bias	12	--- 16thCentury Sleeve.	46
Bias binding	12	Nick or Ditch stitching	21
Binding in	12	Openings, Ideas for	118-9
Binding over	12	Openings, Placing	70
Bodkin	13	Petersham	21
Cartridge pleating	13	Pins	21
Chemise 1450-1500	121-2	Piping	21
Chemise Italian Renaissance	153,158,160	Piping cord	21
Chiffon. Levelling hem	51	Plackard.	123
Control	70	Placket	22
Cutting a Cloak	140-1	Preparing a Hem after fitting.	51
Cutting a Cloak diagram	142	Pressing	23
Cutting a flat front bodice.	113	Pressing seams	23
Cutting and making Foliat dagged sleeves.	161	velvet	31
Cutting long tight sleeves	116	Putting decoration around skirt.	132
Cutting, facings.	132	Quartering, a skirt.	24
Diagonal basting	15	Reinforcing a corner	24
Ditch stitching (see Nick.)	21	Rigilene	24
Domette	15	Scissors	24
Dress making stands or dummies.	35	Sleeve. Adding false puffs into	169
Drill	15	Dolman	61
Edge stitching	15	Hanging	91-97
Eylets	15	Italian Renaissance	161-71
Facing	16	Lining hanging	94
Fastenings	16	Pocketing	59
Buttons and Holes	17	Splayed Seam	50
Hooks and loops	16	Putting two into one armhole	168
Hooks and bars	17	setting fabric in full	164
Hooks and holes	17	distributing fabric in full	164
Lacing	17	Squares	25
Felling or Hemming	18	Stay tape	24
Finishing	18	Stiletto	24
Fitting one side only.	54	Surcoat. Draping on the bias.	135
Flat tacking or Basting	18	Draping on the straight of the grain.	130
Foots width away	19	fastening	138
Fur. Dealing with	32	Fitting a	56
Fusible fabrics	19	Lady Lutrell	63
Gathering	19	Tailor's Chalk	24
Godet	19	Tape	24
Gusset	20	Tracing paper	24
Hem. Piped,	52	Tracing wheel	25
Hemming (see Felling.)	18	Turn out (see Bag.)	11
Hems, Dealing with circular	116	Waistband	25
Hems. How to prepare	51	Wax	25
Herringbone	20	Webbing	25
Houppelande.	77	Wheel piece	25
How to treat Large Pattern pieces.	49	Yard stick	25

ACKNOWLEDGEMENTS

I would like to thank the Witt and Conway Libraries at Courtauld Institute of Art, without whose vast collection of reproductions of paintings and illuminated manuscripts, the drawings in this book would not be so varied.

I am indebted: to Kathryn Turner whose attractive drawings have made the complicated costumes in the source material so easy to understand; also, to Tony Pierce-Roberts who found time in his very busy schedule to photograph plates: 6, ll, 14, 15, 31, 33 - 37, 41 a, b, c, 49 and 54 - 58.

Many thanks to the designers who very kindly allowed me to use their designs; to John Bloomfield who is always so generous, to Nicholas Georgiadis for the loan of the 'Romeo and Juliet' design, and to John Gunter for allowing Kathryn to copy his original.

Again many thanks to Suzi Clarke who reads the drafts, making sure I have not forgotten a vital part of the process. To Marian Florantin, who sadly died in 1994 and who was always a willing researcher. Also, to my long suffering neighbour who helped check page and illustration numbers. For the photographs, many thanks to Guy Gravett for the two 'Tito', and to Ira Nowinski for the three of the fittings. To Demetra at 'Classic Fabric Design' for the loan of one of the 'Romeo and Juliet' photographs.

I would also like to thank both Rosie Runciman and Jane Fenwick from the Glyndebourne Archive who were both so helpfull in finding the 'Pelleas et Melisande' and the Ira Nowinski photograph on page 48.

I would like to thank The Museum of London for the cuff photograph on page 67, and Kay Staniland for allowing Kathryn to draw both the cuff and the 16th century sleeve, Also the National Gallery, London for permission to reproduce 'The Arnolfini Marriage' and 'The Donne Triptch',

Grateful thanks must also go to William-Alan Landes of Players Press, for his encouragement and patience for waiting through 1991 and 1992 all consuming Glyndebourne seasons and his willingness to start editing for a second time, after the Los Angeles earthquake.

Jean Hunnisett   © Photo Copyright, Lynda Southon